THE PAUPER

Georg Simmel

THE PAUPER

Edited and Newly Translated by
SIMONA DRAGHICI, PhD

PLUTARCH PRESS
CORVALLIS, OR

This translation first published in the United States of
America by PLUTARCH PRESS, Corvallis, OR, in 2001.

Originally published in Germany as DER ARME, chapter 7
of SOZIOLOGIE, UNTERSUCHUNGEN ÜBER DIE FORMEN DER
VERGESELLSCHAFTUNG von GEORG SIMMEL
Copyright in German text © 1992 by Suhrkamp, Frankfurt
am Main
Copyright in this English edition, Preface, Postface and Index
© 2001 by Simona Draghici

For information, address the publisher:
PLUTARCH PRESS
P.O. Box 195, Corvallis, OR 97339

Library of Congress Cataloging-in-Publication Data

Simmel, Georg, 1858-1918.
   [Der Arme. English]
   The pauper / Georg Simmel; edited and newly translated by
   Simona Draghici.
      p.cm.
   Includes bibliographical references and index.
   ISBN 0-943045-17-7 (pbk.: alk. paper)
    1. Poverty--Moral and ethical aspects. 2. Poor. 3. Social
   classes. I. Draghici, Simona. II. Title

   HC79.P6 S545 2001
   305.5'69--dc21
                                                    2001059348

Manufactured in the United States of America
Book design and cover by JAY

CONTENTS

EDITOR'S NOTE

In its original German, the present essay bears the title *'Der Arme'*, which in an earlier English translation was rendered as 'The Poor'. In that way, Simmel's emphasis on the individual condition was lost, and the reader was given the impression that it was a whole social class that he was dealing with. Nevertheless, a literal translation such as 'the poor man' carries with it undesirable emotional connotations, as it may mean someone deserving pity or who is despicable, which is not exactly what the author wanted to convey. Consequently, the choice fell upon the noun 'pauper' which needs no qualifier, and leaves little room for ambiguity. In the text, though, wherever no confusion is possible, *'der Arme'* was rendered as 'the poor', to convey the relative human condition of which 'pauper' is the absolute. Furthermore, originally published as Chapter VII of Simmel's *SOZIOLOGIE: Untersuchungen über die Formen der Vergesellschaftung* in Leipzig in 1908, the essay is a reworking of an 1906 article *'Zur Soziologie der Armut'* ('On the Sociology of Poverty'). No attempt however has been made here to compare the two texts. For the present translation the original 1908 text was used, and for editorial purposes, we consulted the text as it appears in volume 11 of *Georg Simmel: Gesamtausgabe*, edited by Otthein Rammstedt, Frankfurt am Main, 1992. Long periods were split into shorter sentences for the sake of clarity. Simmel's notes have been set at the foot of corresponding pages and the editor's, which are numbered, have been relegated at the back of the text proper, which alone has been indexed.

VI

PREFACE

'We may be approaching a period
of economic civil wars comparable to that
of the religious civil wars that followed
the Reformation.' - BERTRAND RUSSELL

Should it be loans or grants? Should it be distributed to churches or social service agencies? Through local governments or through lay charities? Is it a matter of charity or of philanthropy? These are some of the dilemmas that confront the 'aid providers', whether heads of governments or of other corporations. They are real, because charity, compassionate aid, is incompatible with industrial and technological capitalism, not only because of its religious implications, that have nothing to do with the positive materialism and economic determinism of the latter, but also because charity is linked to scarcity, a shortage of goods and services for the satisfaction of certain pressing needs, which technological capitalism is presupposed to have done away with, that being its raison d'être: unbounded economic growth and its corollary, high mass consumption. The technological world is expected not only to satisfy any needs but also to anticipate them, and even to create them from its resourcefulness. So, ultimately, it becomes a matter of supply and demand, of market-regulated exchange: one gives something for which one gets something in return, commensurate with the market value of the object and the service thus rendered. Scarcity makes itself felt when normal demand in the sphere of everyday life cannot be satisfied either because of the absence of offer or because *the demander cannot compensate, has nothing to offer in exchange, either at the time of need or in a foreseeable future. Meant to replace the image of scarcity, which is the accompaniment of natural economy by that of abundance linked to the man-made or artefactual world, technology is unable to deal with the latter otherwise than as an encumbrance to be shaken off. Hence all that talk about putting a man or planting trees on Mars coming from the NASA scientists, or about living in bunkers surrounded by projectors of three-dimensional virtual reality. Modern computing machines may indeed be used to fill deficiencies, make up shortages through 'electronic' transfers, diversions, or other commands, and this has been more widely used than openly admitted, for fear that people might stop using computers altogether. (At the time when the European Union got rid of its old management, it was also discovered that a sum amounting to a billion dollars was missing and could not be accounted for. Nearer home: Medicare and Medicaid electronically defray considerable numbers of bills for services and equipment that have not been nor were meant to be delivered.)*

The economic relation of demand and supply is then translated into rights and obligations, a formula of broad scope, thanks to the ambiguity in circulation between law and morality. Demand becomes right, and the satisfaction of the demand is equated with obligation. Whereas in the feudal times, which we loathe so much, right and obligation were two aspects of the same relation: the granting of a right depended on the fulfilment of an obligation, a recurrent and reinforceable connection, the luminaries of the European eighteenth century severed them, and turned the right

VIII

into a universal. The French phrase 'noblesse oblige' entered circulation as a reminder to those who had been ennobled by Emperor Napoleon I and consequently ignored the very notion of obligation in their efforts to assert their rights. Modern technological society has kept the right a universal, while making the obligation to satisfy it optional, a matter of individual conscience. Hence William Graham Sumner's dictum of 1870's:'What do social classes owe each other? – Nothing.' As a result, actual want satisfaction is treated as an individual matter for which one turns to older institutions based on moral bonds, such as the family, with the moral duties among siblings and between parents and children, fraternities, sects and congregations, interested in preserving the unity and cohesion of the larger group.

Moral duties, though, are likely to be turned from moral into legal obligations enforceable under legal penalty whenever and wherever the preservation of the social fabric is seen as depending on it. With the expansion of social services, those who cannot bring their own contribution are likely by general consensus to be granted only the minimum necessary in order to avoid the destruction of the given social order. In other words, the objective of the providers is not the satisfaction of particular needs, but the maintenance of the collectivity to the extent want left unsatisfied is likely to jeopardize the whole. (Indeed, one of the tactics of dismantling old structures is to persistently increase demands made upon them in the name of social justice in such a way as to exceed the capacity to satisfy them.) By extension, this quandary is replicated in the relations between countries, as they come to be regarded as if they were individual persons belonging to one and the same universal family or culture. (This is not an altogether new stance. It has its roots in the messianic ideologies advocated by various polities throughout the centuries. The United States have displayed it whenever it served the interests of one of their socially significant group or another. It was upheld during Teddy Roosevelt's presidency by the Secretary of State Hay, for instance, in a note of 17 July 1902 addressed to the American chargé d'affaires in Athens, from which the following quotation has been taken: 'It behooves the State to scrutinize most jealously the character of the immigration from a foreign land, and, if it be obnoxious to objection, to examine the causes which render it so. Should those causes originate in the act of another sovereign State, to the detriment of its neighbors, it is the prerogative of an injured State to point out the evil and to make remonstrance; **for with nations, as with individuals, the social law holds good that the right of each is bound by the right of the neighbor'** *[emphasis added].)*

In the last few decades, we have witnessed a new division of countries (or regions), namely between 'rich' and 'poor', in virtue of which the latter may qualify for relief while the former are said to have the 'moral obligation' to provide it.

I do not know how we have arrived at this division, although I suspect it to be associated to a degree with overindebtedness, as some countries became insolvent in the international credit market, thus compromising the whole idea of the world balance of payments. In this sense, it seems to me that the division is more a matter of creditworthiness than of want-related charity, and of an increasing reluctance to take risks in

X

the face of sure loss (in other words, to throw good money after bad), unless the governments of the creditor-countries were willing to guarantee private ventures in the debtor-countries, and that being bad economics for national treasuries, it could be made to pass for charity before the tax-paying public. Besides, the charity motive also serves to maintain access and circumvent interdicts imposed by insolvency. Hence the doctrine of 'moral obligation', according to which investors have no obligation at all to invest unless conditions are right, while the governments of rich countries are held to have both a moral obligation and a political interest in helping those who make real efforts to meet those conditions (that is, are in the 'deserving-poor situation').

In more revolute times, one may be reminded, the division was between Christians and heathens (or pagans), while in the nineteenth century, one used to talk of advanced and primitive societies, with room between for an intermediate category. Simmel himself employed that classification in an anthropological sense, differentiating between more complex or intricate social structures and simpler ones.

If after WWII, during decolonization, the countries of the world were divided according to their ideological orientation, which was essentially linked to forms of ownership, into capitalist, socialist and non-aligned, that classification later yielded to another, in terms of industrialization, namely, of underdeveloped, developing, and developed or industrialized countries.

More recently, as Russia decided to embark upon NEP II, and leave it to the other industrialized countries to pay the expenses necessary to complete the social revolution in the rest of the world, a new classification, more ambiguous and at the same time more inclusive, has become necessary, since national liberation and nationalism in general have become old hat once more, when borders no longer count and figures alone are poor motivation for action. Although economic notions, abundance and scarcity have a stronger existential appeal, and are reflected in the religions of desert peoples, in particular. In the process, the Organization of the United Nations has become a rather expensive umbrella organization for the distribution of international aid in the form of goods and services primarily in the poor regions, as borders tend to shift. The fact that its General Secretary was re-elected un-opposed attests the move away from the political. (Its main ambition is to secure a minimum income of two US dollars a day and a personal computer for everyone on the globe before the end of the decade.)

Aid, that is want satisfaction, as a main principle in the relation between rich and poor nations in modern times, seems to me at least, to have made its debut in the material support given underhand by France and Spain to the American colonies in their decision to withstand British punitive intervention. It was granted in order to spite England and deprive her of what the other two kingdoms thought to be a vast market for foreign goods and a source of enrichment for the sponsoring investors. They were mistaken in their calculations, although the aid did serve its ostensible purpose: to help the colonies obtain their independence. (Perhaps one should also remember that the weightiest argument in favour of one continental congress, and implicitly of the

XII

union of the thirteen former colonies, was its decision to underwrite their separate war debts.) WWI ended in squabbles over repayment of debts, compensations, indemnities, exchange rates and relief through new loans among the former belligerents, while the international financial network came to be dominated by the United States. The latter concluded a separate peace with Germany and pumped her with short-term credits as financial aid meant to stimulate her economy, and which in fact, made life so exciting in Berlin in the twenties. The United States had also been the inventor of a new institution, that of humanitarian foreign aid as embodied at the time by the American Relief Administration. Under Herbert Hoover, it started its work by feeding the hungry Belgians under the German military occupation during WWI, with the consent of the Germans. Nevertheless, as soon as that agency focussed its attention onto the eastern parts of Europe, its offer of aid became conditional. Already in 1917, during the Provisional Government era, an American official delegation, headed by Elihu Root, had gone to St.Petersburg to offer conditional financial and other material assistance, under the watchword: 'no fight, no loan!' The ARA's ouvertures to Russia two years later also came to nothing because the Bolshevik government considered the conditions stipulated by the Americans a flagrant interference in the country's internal affairs, while the civil war was going on, and intended to destroy the emerging political system. Among the conditions were: the cessation of hostilities inside the country; the transportation and distribution of victuals within Russia to be implemented under the ARA supervision, and 'solely under the control of the people of Russia *themselves,' giving full opportunity to the inhabitants of each locality to advise the relief agency about the ways and persons by which the particular communities were to be relieved. Eventually, in the summer of 1921, after the civil war had been won by the Bolsheviks, both the ARA and the Soviet government were willing to reach a compromise of sorts: the Russian Patriarch Tikhon and the writer Maxim Gorky were made to petition the Americans for aid; train carriages were cleaned and put back in service (while the price of railway travel was raised several times), retired generals, economists, former politicians and landowners, as well as cultural personalities were brought forth, some of them being temporarily released from prison, in order to take part in the ever-reorganized committees and commissions of aid to the hungry. The ARA fed the railwaymen and distributed victuals in Russia until the middle of 1923. The ARA's Russian section also ran a program in America, through which it contacted friends and relatives of those who had remained in Russia, offering to collect and deliver their food parcels to the addressees individually. (In that way, the ARA inadvertently helped the Cheka, become GPU in the spring of 1922 and allowed to arrest members of the Bolshevik party as well, to put together lists of potential contacts and enemies abroad, with their correspondents in the country; a widespread network of people thus became suspect of plotting against the socialist regime. In that way, too, the very Patriarch Tikhon became a victim of Soviet justice as soon as the American aid program ended.) In those circumstances, a discerning and pro-western Russian historian and university professor in Moscow could not help writing in his intimate diary on 31*

January 1922: 'America is dealing with the bolsheviks as a rich lord with an indigent drunkard. She is giving them a handout but does not sit them at table with her.'

On the other hand, aware of the symbolic and propagandistic value of international aid, that is aid that ignores political boundaries, the Bolsheviks themselves had sent a shipment of grain with their ambassador Ioffe to the new German government, as a token gesture of proletarian solidarity and brotherhood, in November 1918. It was rejected as fast by its head, the social-democrat Friedrich Ebert. The rebuff stirred up the Bolsheviks' determination to avenge themselves by subverting social-democracy in Germany in every way they could think of, ever since.

Such instances cast light on certain implications which foreign relations may lead to when aid, with its inbuilt ambiguity of self-interest and charitable help, is made their ostensible object. Whether proffered out of ideal motives or from sheer economic and political interests, aid cannot help but reaffirm the superiority-inferiority pattern of the interaction at the individual level. The inequality of the intercourse is made even more blatant by its extraterritoriality, which any protestations to the contrary are unlikely to blot out. The inequality of the intercourse finds compensation in mutual suspicion, contempt and resentment, which in turn are very real obstacles on the way to any genuine and lasting rapprochement. When not an outlet for quick speculative returns, aid on easy terms is granted either in order to induce a desired conduct in the recipient, or as a reward for 'good behaviour,' regardless of, or rather impervious to the latter's motives of interaction and priorities. The recipient will try to offset what he consistently perceives as the donor's hypocrisy to the extent he feels the presumptious conduct of the donor as an injury to his own sovereignty. Through a process of psychological rationalization, he will treat the aid he accepts as a tribute to himself, to dispose of as he thinks fit, and concomitantly as an implicit admission of weakness on the part of the donor who is thus regarded as currying favours. Lenin's apparently contradictory statement:'I request that my vote be added in favour of the acceptance of potatoes and arms from the bandits of Anglo-French imperialism' illustrates this kind of rationalization, all the more necessary as ideologically communism means an abundance of goods and services that makes any formal accountability in the sphere of consumption quite superfluous. And Lenin was painfully aware of the discrepancy between theory and aspirations, on the one hand, and the actual conditions in the field, on the other. In that way, to ask for aid, recognition, credits and trade was turned into an acceptable policy as long as it was made to serve one's interests, and through one, those of the 'social revolution,' but not those of the donor. That was what made Stalin not to pursue an initial application for a six billion dollar loan from the US in 1943 at two-and-a-quarter per cent interest. On the other hand, Stalin's acceptance of the lend-lease formula offered by Roosevelt first to the British during WWII had been made easy for him by its objective and business-like formulation, free of any intent of interference in the Soviet policies, and acknowledging Russia's weight in the war theatre. That gave the latter an opportunity to set aside her compensative threats against the

XVI

imperialistic allies for a time, but not the suspicion and the disdain. The United States had bound themselves by legislation, through the Neutrality Act not to lend to or arm any belligerent, and by the so-called Johnson Act of 1934, not to lend to countries that had defaulted on debts incurred during WWI. Consequently, the lend-lease program was conceived and implemented as compensatory aid, on terms that were to be negotiated at the end of the hostilities. Inside the United States, it was officially presented as a necessity for the defence of the country, while in one of his radio talks, President Roosevelt explained to his fellow Americans that the program was meant to provide the implements of war for others to do the fighting in order 'to keep war away from our country.' Thus moral prescriptions (compensatory aid, among them) were invoked to circumvent legal regulations that curtailed the country's participation in the international arena. On the other hand, the end of the cold war, legitimated in economic doctrinal terms as a transition from guns to butter, first formulated by a Harvard economist, coincided with the emancipation of the Soviet leaders from any inferiority complexes vis-à-vis the rich countries, and their regained confidence in the passive obedience of their people. That made possible the resumption of the old aid policies on an unprecedented scale and with a twist, the recipient as extortionist. Gone the religious intimations of the communism of love, in its proletarian internationalism and solidarity, with its sharing of common provisions, the acceptance of which was to be interpreted as a sign of devotion and implicitly as the recognition of the hegemony of the bestower in the overcoming of the common threat to the brotherhood of fighters, that pre-dates any idea of national sovereignty. Politically, that stance could be reactivated whererver positive materialism fails to provide a needed rallying impetus.

If nowadays indebtedness is apparently the main universal indicator of the division between rich and poor on the global scale, other objective (that is, quantitative) indicators are adduced in its support, main among which are the GDP, considered by itself or divided by the number of people it relates to, as well as the area inhabited by them, and the human development indicator. I do not know what the difference is between the GDP and the GNP, unless one wants to do away with the term 'national', and by that, with the notion of national borders, as well as with the central authority of a national government. The GNP used to be defined as the total value of the goods and services produced in a nation during a specified period of time, usually one year. All those figures may be deflated or inflated at will, but in whatever way their are handled, they still convey the inherent heteronomous arbitrariness which any attempt at consolidation, that is of reducing the distance between the top and the bottom of any such classification list, will not do away with. This becomes even more apparent in the case of the 'human development' indicator. It is a composite which turns from environment and total value of resources to the standard measure-ments of the human inhabitants of the globe considered individually: expectation of life, liter-acy, formal education, and individual purchasing power obtained from the gross domestic product divided by the population density of the area under consideration.

XVIII

By and large, there are two ideological orientations at work in this diffuse struggle for consolidation (and global uniformization): one, centred on social justice, the redistribution of any accumulated wealth whether in the possession of individuals or corporate bodies, governments included, and the other, focussing on the dismantling of the existing infrastructures, held to be deficient, and the erection in their place of others, modelled on plans conceived away from the particular regions and guaranteed to secure the affluence necessary for optimum human development. The two trends do not necessarily converge, nor can one say that they are consequential. Nevertheless, the generic name of 'aid' facilitates and justifies both at the same time: the widest variety of transfers of wealth, whether as goods, services, or simply cash, for the widest range of purposes bypassing cumbersome legislation or acting as a substituent. In this interaction, the intermediaries, those who administer them in the name of the 'donors' (another convenient term with moral overtones, that is used as a generic to cover all those ostensibly grouped at the distributing end of the line) play a significant part in the further redistribution of resources as administrative costs and consultancy fees. (They are the sutlers of the modern campaigns of globalization.) The unsteadiness of the aid flow that passes through what is but a service industry, as well as the variety of its sources makes the competition among the various agencies all the more intense, bringing about a never-ending reorganization (often called 'change' or 'reform'), redeployment, reorientation of objectives and personnel, as everybody wants a share of the unpredictable bonanza. The basic mechanism has been tellingly described by Charles Dickens in his novel DAVID COPPERFIELD, in the episode in which on his way to school near London, David is served lunch by a waiter at a hotel in Yarmouth.

If love of one's fellow human beings is what allegedly motivates international aid, under that aspect, it extensively exploits the idealism and spirit of nihilistic self-sacrifice of young and less young people on the look out for ends and causes that are worthy opportunities for the redemption of others through the unpleasantness and the hardships to which they are willing to submit themselves. On the other hand, its rationalization by hired experts whose services are sought to secure the greatest efficiency, absolves the donors of any responsibility in the name of the impersonal objectivity of science and so allows them to maintain their moral superiority, as well, in any confrontation between rich and poor. Ultimately, all the trends, claims and counter-claims with their cross purposes seem set to let the communism of abundance yield to the communism of scarcity which settles for the minimum necessary for the maintenance of life.

*

What has Georg Simmel, who wrote his essay on the pauper almost a hundred years ago, to do with all this? There are a couple of things. First of all, his thinking is that of the era of technology in which socialism and liberalism were still meeting at their common source, which we now try to recover after we have come to recognize the political motivation of the twentieth-century schisms. Secondly, as said earlier, our approaches to world affairs tend to closely

XX

approximate the ways in which we are dealing with each other, at home, within our confines. In other words, for more than a century we have been transposing what is applicable to individuals in conditions familiar to us onto the international field by a kind of reductionism; and that trend or inclination is not peculiar to the Americans alone, despite the publicity. Furthermore, we are dealing with poverty and those affected by it in economic categorial terms, at the expense of other factors, in the name of equality or equality of opportunity, which in practice has always been understood to mean the mental capacity and the tenacity or resoluteness freely to exploit every chance of profit for the sake of profit. The caveat emptor principle is used to justify the licence. (Thus, for instance, when a youngster in the State of New Jersey gained seventy-five thousand dollars in one day through stock manipulation on his computer, he became the media's hero and not only the object of his parents' pride.) Simmel was interested in the fate of the individual, living as subject and also as object in society, the technological society that is still with us; in the apparent and the substantive aspects of the corresponding interrelations; in the process that had led to the modern world with its administrative centralization and rationalization of resources that discount poverty from its calculation. Besides, Simmel has been one of the last beneficiaries of the nineteenth-century liberalism that did not interfere with inquisitiveness, the need of clarification and systematization of knowledge for the sake of knowledge, and of meaning which for some, among whom Simmel, was what gave life its worth. This is very much unlike the 'neo-liberalism' of today, which perpetuates the

XXI

inclination of the twentieth century, namely of the purposeful cultivation of fogginess and confusion behind everyday discourse made up of watch-words, which we now call soundbites, in order to condition 'the masses' to accept or at least not to resist their leaders' mental deficiencies. Simmel himself was aware of this trend when he was quipping 'thinking hurts'. Still another reason to turn to Simmel for enlightenment is that unlike all the present authors who write about poverty and poor people from their position of intermediaries and objective observers, Simmel lived it and made use of his powers of reflection to uncover its significance in a secular, industrialized world. The fact that his references were chosen from among the legislative decisions of the nineteenth century and earlier does not negate the continued validity of the principles and of the reasoning behind them, rather it enables us to assess what progress we have made in this direction, if any.

The 'transnational liberal order' at the end of the twentieth century, like its nineteenth-century model, is keen on separating the individual from and pit him against society (the 'human development' indicator mentioned above is part of the evidence), and in this way, the latter becomes 'civil'. Concomittantly, this neo-liberal order is inclined to resolve any conflict, emerging from this separation, in a court of law, on the basis of alleged or prescribed rights or obligations. Moreover, as borders cease to count, universal jurisdiction is what law courts the world over aspire to. Quite topically, Simmel starts his essay with an examination of their meaning in their shifting relation to the individual qua human being, that is as person with a distinct separate existence which is an end in itself. It serves as a preamble to the

XXII

analysis of the narrower subject matter of want satisfaction within their framework. Want, the absence of means to a certain end, is the essential characteristic that distinguishes the condition of being poor from any other not only in purely personal and psychological terms but also of social intercourse, which render it relative. In the modern industrial society, want satisfaction ceases to be a right of the individual poor or pauper because he ceases to be the ultimate purpose of relief. As the title of the essay announces, Simmel concentrates on the needy individual in the many-sided relationships which develop between him and society on various planes and from different angles, subjective and objective, apparent and substantive, in interpersonal, in-group, community and modern centralized federal state contexts, respectively. He warns us of the need to distinguish between poverty as a social deficiency that demands relief and presents the community with the task of giving the least chance to various handicaps and circumstances to result in impoverishment, on the one hand, and the individual condition, which ultimately is the insufficiency of means for a person's ends (p.46), on the other. In that way, he also makes us aware of the reason why poverty is not eliminated by relieving the poor individually, and also understand why there where poverty is prevalent, the individual may not necessarily consider himself poor. The conflict between want satisfaction as charity versus social service is complicated by the variety of standards by which want itself is determined and relief meted out, and their ineffectiveness in dealing with personal needs outside those limits. Hence, in the modern technological society, between the haves and have-nots as donors and recipients, respectively, there is a persistent gap which the intermediaries only broaden by their growing number. Nonetheless, in that process, the pauper is not rid of his social role, which after all is that of receiving help, but to the contrary, that role grows in importance with the growing number of intermediaries.

*

For the translator, though, Simmel's present essay is not unproblematic, unlike other texts of his. A social liberal himself, Simmel had accumulated first-hand experience, material, moral and psychological, of involuntary want in a Germany that after a slump in the fifties, had set upon the road of recovery to reach the zenith of industrialization and prosperity by the end of the century, developing in the bargain the most advanced social welfare system in the industrial world at the time. The intricacies of his long periods may reflect his wrestling with an unruly profusion of related observations and his sustained intellectual effort to attain a clarity of vision which a critical examination of any subject matter required but was not easy to achieve when dealing with a social condition that could also be a source of pain and distress as much as an object of pity and self-pity. Whatever the reasons for the unwieldy prose, the challenge which it presents is as rewarding: forced to disentangle threads and knots and trace links and ends from the ball of Simmel's representation of the world, one discovers meanings and insights which fluent discourse would have passed over. It is the connections in context that the interpreter must pay attention to and not just to the words as they are set one after the

XXIV

other, and both translators and readers are inter-preters, in the first place. By this I do not want to dismiss an earlier translation that was printed in the journal SOCIAL PROBLEMS in 1965 (vol. 13, No. 2) as worthless, far from it, given the difficulties, just mentioned, in the original text. It is apparent that for the author of that translation, Simmel's philosophy remained a secret, and that made her feel ill at ease with the text through-out. By necessity her English version turned out ponderous and obscure, condemned to remain buried in the periodical in which it was printed, while Simmel's ideas came to be falsely attributed to others.

What Simmel would attempt in his labour of reflection was to cast a bridge between the social and the individual by insisting that while no man is an island, nor is he the abject and exclusive product of the collectivity either. In the second footnote appended to the text (pp. 40–41), he outlines the interaction between the individual and society, underlines the part played by the latter in the formation of one's personality, and at the same time, the role of the individual as mediator between the varigated forces that impinge on him and society. He points to their common ground-work and their actual manifestations, in which the weight of the impact of each upon the other oscillates in favour either of the individual or the social, without ever attaining a complete split between the two. Society, or the collectivity, acts in two ways upon the individual: one, in direct confrontation, in the day-to-day existence, and the other, by providing the apriorities that con-stitute the foundation of individual development, the unity of the whole that finds expression in individual diversity which in turn gives it its

dynamism by re-stating the meanings of its forms. This is possible because of man's unique ability to contemplate himself as subject and object simultaneously in an all embracing perception as if he were a third person. (Because this ability is not fully developed in each and every one of us, it will be an irreparable error to dismiss it as irrelevant.) Hence also Simmel's definition of reality as 'a mode of experiencing, a form that gives shape to contents.' Relatedly, his moral philosophy is but a subjective form of inquiry into the relationship between the individual, both as object and subject, and the social (implicit in norms, customs and laws). He would select those elements or segments of reality from the aggregate of social life, which by their operations appeared to him to bear upon the particular problem or object of analysis with which he was concerned at the time. From the connections traced by him in his investigation, Simmel would reveal the real-life interactions that form the content of, or are essential to, the matter in question from the position which he had adopted in his inquiry. That position is sociological only to the extent the core of his approach is interactional. So it will be wrong to consider him a sociologist for that matter. (There was nothing to prevent him from changing his perspective in keeping with his object of inquiry.) At the same time, while not hostile to positivism as a method of investigation, he was aware of its limitations to explain human conduct that is essentially non-logical, and was against its generalization and its reification into a dogma of progress, with its emphasis on prediction, empirical verifiability, and its ultimate aim: to obtain the perfect social form. While appropriating and integrating the findings
XXVI

*of experimental psychology in his own philosoph-
ical inquiry, his search for meaning does not
dispense with the metaphysical either, while
allowing him to consider no object in the immediate too trivial or too insignificant for consideration. He has enabled us in this way to see not
only how norms emerge, that regulate intercourse
and acquire a life of their own, but also how in
practical life, they retain the doubleness or duplicity which may be deceitfully exploited, although
as such it implies no deceit.*

March 1998 - October 2000   Simona Draghici

THE PAUPER

As far as man is considered a human being, to every obligation of his corresponds a right of another human being. Perhaps conceptually, it would be more insightful to think that at the beginning there were only rights, and that each individual has his own requirements, which in general are human but also result from his particular condition. They are rights as such only when they become the obligations of the other. Nevertheless, as everyone who becomes duty-bound in this manner has also rights anyway, a network of rights and obligations develops, in which the right however is the primary element that sets the tone. The obligation, on the other hand, is merely its correlate, although unavoidable indeed as part of the same act.

By and large, society may be regarded as an interaction of human beings that have moral, legal, conventional, and still many other kinds of rights. That the latter constitute but obligations for the others is only a logical or technical consequence, so to speak. If the unthinkable could happen, and everyone's right might be satisfied otherwise than as an obligation, then society would no longer need the category of obligation. By taking a radical stand, in the sense of an ideal ethical construct, that still might be possible, although certainly it would no longer correspond to the psychological reality: all the acts of love and compassion, of generosity and religious impulse would be interpreted as **rights** of the beneficiaries. Against all those motivations ethical rigour has already asserted that the most one can do is to fulfil one's duty, and this requires from oneself what to a lackadaisical or self-adulatory character appears as merit, above any obligation. And from that rigour there is only one step: to set the right of the claimant behind the gratifier's obligation. This seems indeed the ultimate and most rational postulate for one's services to the other. Here, though, a fundamental contradiction becomes now apparent between the sociological[1] and the ethical categories. To the extent the interaction is the consequence of a law, in the broadest meaning of the word, which includes the juridical, the man-to-man relationship has fully permeated the moral values of the individual and determines their direction. All the same, the unquestioned idealism of this point of view stands in contrast to the no less deep-seated rejection of every inter-individual genesis of obligation: our obligations are obligations towards our very selves, and that is all. As regards their **contents**, they may aim our conduct conduct at the other, but we cannot derive their form and motivation from them: rather, obligations arise from the self and its unmixed inner needs as pure autonomy, fully independent of anything outside. Only in the context of the law is the other the terminus a quo[2] of the motivation in our moral actions. For morals as such, though, the opposite applies, namely the terminus ad quem.[3] In the last analysis, only we ourselves are responsible for the morality of our acts. We are responsible to our better selves, our self-esteem, or whatever one may call that mysterious focal point which ultimately the soul finds in itself as its last instance, and from which it decides freely the extent to which the rights of the other are his obligations.[4]

2

The different interpretations of the relief of the poor may serve as an illustration or empirical symbol of this dualism of principles in the basic sentiments about the purport of the moral act. The obligation to provide relief may appear as the very correlate of the claim made by the poor themselves. Particularly in those countries where begging is a regular occupation, the beggar more or less naively believes that he has a right to the handout. On the other hand, he often reproves its denial as a withholding of a tribute owed to him. An entirely different trait--within the same category--justifies the claim to relief on the grounds of group affiliation of the needy. A social conception, that considers the individual as being entirely the product of his societal surroundings, grants to each the right to compensation from the latter for every hardship and loss. Even there where one does not come across such a complete elimination of individual responsibility, stress may still be laid, from a social standpoint, on the right of the needy as the basis of all assistance to the poor. Only then when such a right is assumed, albeit as a mere social-legal fiction, is poor relief shielded from arbitrariness, from dependence on a chance financial situation, and the usual uncertainties. Everywhere the reliability of the functions would increase whenever in the correlation between right and obligation, the former is the starting point, methodologically speaking. After all, on an average, the human being is more readily disposed to demand a right than to fulfil an obligation. Besides, there is a humanitarian motive involved: the demand for and the acceptance of relief by the poor weigh less on the minds of the poor when they are considered the positive result of their right. The dejection, the shame, the loss of status inherent in alms-giving are overcome to the extent the alms are not granted out of compassion, a sense of duty or just expediency, but are to be laid claim to by the poor. Well, this right obviously has its own limits which must be determined in each individual case. In this way, the right to relief will not change them in their material-quantitative respect, in relation to other motivations. Only its inner meaning will be laid down by that to become a fundamental notion about the relationship between one individual and another, and between the individual and the whole community. The right to relief belongs in the same category as the right to work, as the right to life. The vagueness of the quantitative limits that characterizes these and other 'human rights' reaches its maximum without doubt in each and every case, particularly when the relief is in cash. Then the objective delimitation of the claim is complicated by the purely quantitative and relative character of money even more than it is when the relief is rendered in kind. Save in complex or highly individualized cases, in which the poor may indeed put an aid in cash to better and more profitable use than the relief in kind with its provident character. Likewise, it is in no way clear at whom the right of the poor is aimed in reality.[5] The resolution of this problem reveals deep socio-logical differences. A poor man who feels that his condition is an injustice of the world order, and asks for help from life as a whole, so to speak, will easily hold each and every individual who is better off than he responsible for his claim, out of solidarity. Such an attitude is readily amenable to scaling: from the deliquent proletarian who sees his enemy in every well-dressed person, the

4

representative of the class that has disinherited him, and whom he robs with a clear conscience for that very reason, and on to the humble beggar who entreats for a donation 'for God's sake', as though each human being were duty-bound to fill the holes of the order which God aspired to but has not fully managed to complete. The demand of the pauper is here directed to the individual, yet not to someone in particular. It is made rather on the grounds of the solidarity of humankind in general. Beyond this correlation, which permits every individual to be a representative of the whole of existence with respect to the claims addressed to it, there are the well-demarcated, particular collectivities to which the claims of the poor may be directed. The State, the community, the parish, the professional association, the circle of friends, the family, all may as totalities maintain extremely varied relations with their members. Nonetheless, each of these relations seems to include an element which is actualized as the right of the individual to relief in the event of his impoverishment. This is the common feature of such sociological relations which in other respects are quite heterogeneous. The claims of the poor originating in such ties are characteristically mixed under primitive conditions. There, tribal customs and religious obligations, in an undifferentiated unity, have a commanding influence on the individual. Among the ancient Semites, the claim of the poor to share a meal had not personal generosity as its correlate but rather social affiliation and religious practice.[6] The right of the poor is brought into greater prominence wherever poor relief is grounded in an organic union of the elements, whether the union is religious, deriving from a metaphysical unity, tribal, or familial, as it goes back to the biological unity. On the other hand, there where poor relief is teleologically[7] dependent on a goal that is attainable through it, rather than being a consequence of a real and effective fellowship, the right of the poor to make demands is reduced to nil.[8]

In the cases discussed so far, right and obligation have appeared only as the two sides of an absolute relationship. Nevertheless, new tendencies become evident as soon as the starting point shifts from the right of the recipient to the obligation of the donor. In an extreme case, the poor disappear entirely as legitimate subjects and foci of interest. The motive of the donation lies exclusively in the significance which the latter assumes for the donor. When Jesus said to the wealthy young man: give your possessions to the poor, what obviously mattered to him were not the poor at all, but the soul of the young man for whose salvation every renunciation was only the means or the symbol. The later Christian alms were of the same nature: nothing but a kind of ascesis or 'good works' that improves the fate of the donor beyond the grave.[9] The inordinate expansion of mendicancy in the Middle Ages, the senseless use made of gifts, the demoralization of the proletariat through indiscriminate charities that counteract all civilizing work[10]--all these are the revenge, so to speak, which the alms take on the purely subjective motive of the handout that takes into consideration the donor only, but not the recipient. As soon as the welfare of the whole society requires that the poor be aided, the motivation limited to the giving subject is discarded without for that matter any attention being paid to the recipient.

6

Consequently, the relief is either voluntary or enforced by law in order to discourage the poor from becoming the active and destructive enemies of society, and instead, render their diminished energies productive once more, and prevent the degeneration of their progeny.[11] The poor as persons, their awareness of their own condition, remain as indifferent in this case as when alms are given for the salvation of one's soul. The subjective selfishness implicit in the latter case is put an end to but not for the sake of the poor, rather for the sake of society. That the poor receive the donation is not its ultimate aim but just a means as in that instance. The prevalence of the social standpoint with regard to alms is made evident by the fact that they may be refused from the same viewpoint.[12] In fact this often happens when personal compassion or the unpleasantness of saying no would move us to give.

Accordingly, poor relief as a public institution assumes the aspect of a highly characteristic sociological constellation. Its contents are thoroughly personal: it lightens individual plight if anything. It is what distinguishes it from other institutions the object of which is public safety and welfare. All the citizens want to benefit from the other institutions: the army and the police, schools and public works, justice and church, popular representation and the pursuit of science. In principle, they do not cater for particular individuals but rather for their sum. The aim of these institutions is the unity of the many or of all. On the other hand, in its practices, poor relief concentrates on the individual and his condition, exclusively. This very individual becomes the terminus, the end of the line, so to speak, of the modern, abstract form of poor relief, but absolutely not its **ultimate end**. The latter consists much more in the protection and the advancement of the community.[13] Not once can the poor be referred to as **a means** to that end--which would only improve their position. Social action does not make use of them as such, but only as certain objective means, material and administrative, for the elimination of the implicit threatening dangers and losses which the poor represent for the welfare of the community. This formal constellation obviously is valid not only for the collectivity in general, but also for the narrower circles. Even within the family, countless acts of relief are done less to benefit the recipients than not to put the family to shame and damage its reputation just because of the poverty of one of its members. The unemployment benefits granted by the English trade unions to their members are not meant to relieve individual want as much as to prevent the unemployed from working for less, out of necessity, and so force down the standard wages for the trade. It becomes clear from this meaning of poor relief that taking from the well-to-do to give to the poor does not in any way lead to the equalization of their individual positions. Nor does it neutralize the **tendency** to divide society into rich and poor. On the contrary, it is grounded in the structure of society, as it is in fact. It stands in the sharpest contrast to all socialist and communist endeavours to abolish this social structure.[14] The purpose of poor relief is precisely to attenuate the extremes of social differentiation in such a way as to allow every social structure to rest on this differentiation. Were the interests of the individual poor at the basis of the relief, no limits would be imposed upon that principle by which the transfer

8

of assets in his favour would be hampered before equalization were achieved. Instead, there are the interests of the whole society, of the political, familial and other socially determined circles, that lie at its basis. Hence there is no reason to extend to the poor more assistance than it is required to maintain the status quo of the respective totality.

Wherever this purely social centralistic teleology is at work, poor relief produces the greatest sociological tension between the direct and the indirect objectives of any action. The attenuation of the subjective need is emotionally so categorial an end in itself that to deprive it of its ultimate purpose and reduce it to a mere technique for the transsubjective ends of a social entity represents an outstanding triumph of the latter. The distance that grows between the social entity and the individual is, despite its inconspicuousness, more fundamental and radical in its detached and abstract character than the self-sacrifices of the individual for the collectivity in which the means and ends are cultivated in such a way as to combine into one emotional order.[15]

The complexity of rights and obligations that is characteristic of the modern State relief of the poor finds its explanation in this basic sociological relationship. In many a situation we are faced with the principle according to which the State has the obligation to assist, but the poor have no corresponding right to assistance. As it has been made quite clear, the poor in England, for instance, cannot sue for damages if they are illegally denied assistance.[16] In this respect the whole relationship between rights and obligations is overlooked. The right corresponding to that obligation of the State is not the poor's but of each and every citizen that pays taxes for the poor to an extent and in such a way as to attain the public goal of the relief truly and effectively. As a result, the poor have no right to sue for negligence in the distribution of the relief. Only the other elements of the collectivity, indirectly affected by the negligence, can do so. Thus, for example, were one able to prove that a thief would have refrained from a robbery, had he been granted the lawful relief withheld from him, then the victim of the robbery would in principle be entitled to claim compensation from the welfare administration.[17] In the legal teleology, the relief of the poor assumes the same status as the protection of animals. In Germany, nobody is punished for an injury caused to an animal unless it has been done 'publicly or in an offensive manner'. Thus, not the mistreated animal but rather respect for the witnesses of the mistreatment is what justifies the punishment. This exclusion of the poor guarantees them no purposive link in the teleological chain, nor is it, as we have seen, at work inside the modern, relatively democratic State. It is only in this sector of public administration that the persons who are essentially interested in public relief have no part to play in it. Poor relief, even in the interpretation given above, is only the spending of public means for public ends, and there, away from the poor, lies its entire teleology. That does not happen in the case of the parties that have an interest in other administrative matters. Hence, the principle of auto-administration, which is still more or less observed in other sectors, does not apply in the case of the poor and of poor relief. When the State is under a more or less statutory obligation to divert a stream in order to secure the irrigation of certain areas, the stream is

10

somewhat in the situation of the poor supported by the State: the stream is admittedly the object of the obligation but it does not carry the right that corresponds to that obligation; the right rather belongs to the owners of the land contiguous to the stream. Each time this exclusively centralist interest prevails, the right-obligation relationship may also change according to the standpoint from which the purpose is considered. Prussia's 1842 Draft of the Poor Law stresses that the State must assume the implementation of the relief of the poor in the interest of the general welfare. To that end, it created legal public bodies that were committed to the State to support the needy individuals. They were not meant to commit themselves to the latter, because the needy had no right to legal claims. Situations like these come to a critical point there where the State law imposes the obligation to provide alimentation for the needy on their better-off relatives.[18] At first sight it appears that the poor have in fact a claim on their more affluent relatives, which the State undertakes to safeguard and enforce. The inner meaning, though, is another. The State commonwealth takes care of the poor for motives of expediency, and in turn shifts off the support to the relatives, either because the costs would be exorbitant, or at least are thought to be so. The law does not concern itself with any direct demand from person to person as it may at times happen between the worse-off brother and his prosperous sibling. That is a purely moral obligation. The law has exclusively to look after the interests of the collectivity, and it does so from both sides: by assisting the poor, and by collecting the expenses from their relatives. This is the sociological structure of the nutrition laws. They are not intended merely to lend the compelling form of law to moral obligations. This has been made clear in the preceding lines, and will also become obvious in what follows. Certainly, the moral claim to support between siblings is by far more exacting. Nevertheless, when an attempt was made to give it legal sanction in the first draft of the Civil Code, the motives set forth readily acknowledged the implicit harshness, but gave as grounds for its inclusion the too elevated costs which otherwise would be incurred by the public care of the poor. It even made evident that the legal obligation of maintenance often exceeds the limit that might be required individually from a moral point of view.[19] The Imperial Court of Justice has ruled against an impecunious old man, ordering him to surrender all that he possessed-- several hundred marks--for the upkeep of his son, incapable of gainful employment, although he argued convincingly that he himself would soon be incapable of gainful employment, and that the money in question was his only reserve. It is extremely doubtful whether in this case one may still speak of the son's moral right. The public, though, do not ask themselves this question, but only whether they can be indemnified for their obligation towards the poor in keeping with the generally valid norms. The deeper meaning of the obligation to the alimentation aid is conveyed eloquently by the practical course which it takes. Firstly, the poor are helped to submit their applications; then, sons or fathers are looked for, and eventually fined, in order to make good if not all the costs of the relief, at least half or a third, out of their own pockets, in keeping with their means. Thus, the exclusively social meaning of the

12

measure is made apparent by the fact that the alimentation aid provided for in the Civil Code is made available only whenever it does not 'jeopardise' the 'social status' of those under the obligation to extend it. It is questionable, to say the least, whether an aid incurring such a risk in certain cases would be morally required. Nevertheless, the public forgo it in any case, so long as an individual's fall from his social rung is detrimental to the fabric of society, which seems to outweigh in social importance the material advantages derived by extorting everyone. The former is nothing else but the obligation of the State which has thrust it upon the relatives, and which in fact needs no corresponding right on the part of the poor.

Indeed, the above-mentioned parable of the diverted stream was inaccurate to the extent the poor are not only poor but citizens as well. As such, they certainly share in the rights which the law grants to all the citizens as correlate of the obligation incumbent on the State to assist the poor. By making use of the same parable, let us say that the poor are the stream and its contiguous landowners at one and the same time, in the same way as the wealthiest citizens. Formally, indeed, the functions of the State stand at the same ideal distance from all the citizens. Nonetheless, in keeping with individual conditions, they have very diverse meanings as regards their contents. When for that reason the poor are associated with the obligation to the poor, they act not as subjects with their own goals, but only as members of the teleological organization of the State which transcends them. Thus their role, so to speak, in that function of the State is quite different from that of the well-to-do. Whereupon

13

one becomes aware that sociologically the whole, materially induced peculiarity of the situation of the assisted poor does not prevent them from being members of the State entity. This happens despite the fact that their overall situation makes of their condition the superficial objective of an action of relief, and that they are treated as inert objects without rights within the overall intentionality of the State. Notwithstanding both these tendencies which seem to place the poor outside the State, or more correctly by the means of which the poor enmesh themselves organically within the network of the whole, the poor belong as poor to the historical reality of society which lives in them and above them. They are as much a formal sociological element as the civil servants or the tax-payers, the schoolteachers or the tradesmen. The poor are more or less in the situation of the stranger who also stands objectively, so to speak, outside the group with which he stays.[20] Even in this case, though, the image of a whole emerges, comprising the autonomous parts of the group along with the stranger. The particular interactions between the group and the stranger create the larger group and determine the true historical circle.[21] Thus the poor are indeed situated outside the group to a certain extent, but this is only a particular kind of interaction which interweaves them with the whole in the broadest sense of the term.

The sociological antinomy of the poor resolves itself only by this way of looking at the facts, to the extent it reflects the social-ethical difficulties inherent in the relief of the poor. The solipsistic tendency of the medieval type of alms, of which I spoke already, went past the poor, inwardly. The action had only an outward value, according to which the other people should not be treated as mere tools, but always simultaneously, as an end. In principle, in such circumstances, the recipient is a giver as well: a reactive beam gets from him back to the donor, and this is exactly what turns the gift into an interaction, into a sociological event. Nevertheless, if as in the preceding case, the recipient is excluded altogether from the end-process of the giver, he plays no role but that of a box in which a donation has been dropped for some mass for the dead. In that way the interaction is cut short, and the donation is no longer a social event but merely an individual act.[22] Now, to be sure, it appears that the modern public administration does not deal with the relief of the poor as an end in itself either. Nonetheless, it alone expresses the fact that the poor, standing as they do in the teleological sequence which excludes them, belong organically to the whole, and on this very basis, are woven into the end-process. Certainly, in this case too, their reaction to the gift that comes their way has as little individual feedback as it had in all the medieval instances. It is the totality of the social sphere alone that in its turn practically experiences a feedback to what it has done for the poor by rehabilitating their economic activity, preventing their physical deterioration and deflecting their impulse to get rich through violence. A purely individual relationship will be ethically adequate and sociologically complete only when truly each individual is a reciprocal end for the other--although naturally, not only an end. This does not apply however to the actions of the suprapersonal collectivity. With its teleology, such a collectivity may easily aim beyond the individual and return to itself, without tarrying at him, so to speak. As far as every individual belongs to this whole, he is placed thereby at the final point of the action, from the start, and is not, as in the other case, left outside it. On the contrary, as a member of the whole, he shares in the end-in-itself character of the whole, as the result of the same **direct** denial of his own end-in-itself character. Solid signs of the organic role, played in the life of the collectivity by this centralist view of the nature of poor relief, had made themselves felt long before its clear prevalence. Thus, in the England of old, poor relief came from monasteries and ecclesiastical corporations, and as it will be made evident, for the very fact that property in mortmain alone had the reliable continuance, on which poor relief depended in absolute terms. The various secular gifts from spoils and donations given as penance did not make up for it, because they could not yet find a place in the administrative system, and so were likely to be expended without any lasting effect. Thus poor relief linked itself directly to the only substantially firm point in the societal jumble and upheavals.[23] That link showed itself in a negative way in the indignation against the clergy sent to England from Rome, because they overlooked the relief of the poor. The foreign cleric did not feel himself intimately bound to the life of the community, and his indifference to the poor appears as the most obvious sign of the divide. The same connection between the relief of the poor and the stablest substratum of social existence reappeared clearly in England in the subsequent linkage of the poor tax to landed property. That was as much the cause as the effect of the fact that the poor counted as a stable organic part of the land. The same tendency was confirmed once more as late as

16

1861, when some of the burden was legally transferred from the parish to the welfare association of the poor.[24] The costs of the relief were no longer to be covered entirely by the parish, but were to be defrayed from a fund to which the parish had to contibute in proportion to the value of its landed properties. The proposal that the allocation should have also taken into account the number of the inhabitants had been repeatedly and explicitly rejected. In that way, the individualistic element was eliminated. The sum total of persons appeared no longer as the upholder of the obligation to the poor. It was the suprapersonal entity with its underlying basis in the materiality of land and soil that assumed that role. In those circumstances, the relief of the poor was so central to the social group that it became the focal point of the local administration long before education, public works, public health and the registry office. Elsewhere too, as a result of its success, the public administration of poor relief became a direct factor of state centralization and uniformization. The North German Confederation decided that no needy person should be left without relief within its boundaries, and that no poor North German should be subjected to different treatments in different regions of the Confederation. Whereas in England, where the connection between relief and landed property was built on an objectively technical basis, it did not change its deeper sociological meaning. On the other hand, when it came to cross county borders, the addition of other sectors to the public administration showed considerable technical disadvantages because of the welfare associations of the poor. By this very fact, the contradiction in its technical meaning, more than in anything else, throws into bold relief the unity in its sociological aspect. For that reason it is entirely one-sided to describe poor relief as 'an organization of propertied classes for the fulfilment of the moral obligations associated with ownership'. It is much more a part of the organization of the **whole**, to which the poor belong just as much as the propertied classes. It is as certain that the technical and material particulars of their social position represent them as mere objects or crossing points in a collective life that goes beyond them. Ultimately, it is as certain, generally speaking, that the role of each and every concrete member of society is valued according to a point of view temporarily adopted here, namely what Spinoza was saying about God and the individual: we may love God, indeed, but it would be inconsistent that He, the whole that contains us, should love us in turn; the love which we give Him is much more a part of the infinite love with which God loves Himself. The singular exclusion from the community which maintains them, and which the poor experience, is the expression of their role **within** society, as its oddly situated members. In so far as technically they are mere objects of society, sociologically they are subjects, who like others, constitute that social reality, on the one hand, and on the other, find themselves, like all the rest, on the far side of its suprapersonal, abstract entity.

For that reason, the overall structure of the group must provide an answer to the following question: where do the poor belong? In so far as they still carry on some economic activity, they belong to that sector of the general economy in which they are directly involved. As far as they are members of a church, they belong to it

18

without any kind of restrictions from other similar venues. To the extent they are members of a family, the poor belong to the personal and spatially well-circumscribed circle of their relatives. But as such, where do the poor belong? A society, that is held together or is organized on the basis of tribal awareness, places the poor inside the circle of their tribe. In another group, whose ethical links are in the main mediated by the Church, this or the religious associations are the scene of society's reaction to the factual presence of the poor. The motive of the 1871 German law on the place of residence for those on relief answers the question in the following way: the poor belong to that community, that is to say the community liable to support them, which has benefitted by their economic capacity before their impoverishment. According to that principle, by designating as the community any locality that had enjoyed the economic output of those now impoverished, the social structure showed itself as it had been before the complete victory of the idea of the modern State. The free movement in modern times, the interlocal exchange of productive forces has removed this restriction, so that the whole State federation is alone considered the terminus a quo and ad quem[25] of all activities. Nowadays, as a State law permits to all and sundry to reside in any community they like, the integrating relation between the community and its residents disappears. In the absence of the right to oppose the settlement of undesirable persons in the community, the latter can no longer rely on the solidary, give-and-take relationship with the individual. Only for practical reasons, and only as organ of the State--the same legal motives go on emphasizing--does the community take over the care of the poor.[26] This is the extreme point reached by the formal position of the poor, revealing its dependency on the overall stage of societal development. The poor belong to the largest operational circle. They are not part of the whole, but rather the whole, to the extent it forms a unity, is a place or power, where the poor belong as long as they are poor. Because it is the largest, this circle has nothing outside it to which to pass the obligation.[27] It alone does not experience the difficulty stressed by relief workers inside small associations: these would repeatedly refuse assistance to a needy person for that particular reason, afraid as they are that once they busy themselves with him, they would have him hanging like a millstone round their necks for ever. A characteristic trend, with a strong effect on human socialization, becomes apparent in such cases. It may be called moral induction: in other words, when a good turn is done, of whatever kind, even the most spontaneous and unusual, not dictated by any obligation, the doer actually feels it to be his duty to persist, independently of the beneficiary's expectations.[28] It is an utterly trivial life experience, but a beggar, who has been given alms regularly, comes in no time to regard it as his right and the donor's obligation. If the latter stops his handouts, his action is censured as if it were the evasion of a tax due to the beggar who for that reason feels such anger as he would hardly feel against anyone who has always refused to give him anything. On the other hand, anyone in better circumstances, who has been aiding a needy person for some time, having settled the duration of the aid beforehand, will nonetheless end it with a feeling of distress, as if he had

20

begun it from an obligation.[29] A Talmudic law, in the ritual code Jore Deah, acknowledges it in all awareness: whoever has aided a poor man three times by handing him the same amount of money on each occasion, tacitly assumes the obligation to continue his aid even if he has no intention to do so. The action takes on the character of a vow from which he may desist only for exceptional reasons (such as, for instance, his own impoverishment). This case is much more complicated than the related instance that forms the complement to odisse quem laeseris,[30] namely to love the one to whom one had done a good turn. By this, understandably, one projects the satisfaction derived from the good deed upon the person who has offered the opportunity to carry it out. One loves oneself essentially in the love for the person for whom one has made a sacrifice, as one hates oneself in the hatred one feels towards the person whom one has wronged. The above-mentioned peculiar form of noblesse oblige,[31] cannot be explained by such a simple psychology. I believe that an a priori condition is in fact at work here: that every action of this kind--in spite of its apparently absolute voluntariness and obvious character of opus supererogationis[32]-- results from an obligation. Furthermore, all such actions presuppose a deeper-lying obligation which to a degree is rendered palpable in them. It happens as in the case of theoretical induction, which accepts the similarity between a past course of events and a future course not simply because the nature of the former was this or that, but rather because a **law**[33] may be drawn from it, which determines that course as much as it must determine any future event. Hence a moral instinct must be at its root, according to which the first good deed already presupposes an obligation, and that in turn requires another obligation, no smaller than the first. Obviously, all this is connected with the motives mentioned at the beginning of this chapter. If all the sacrifices, all the good deeds and all the selflessness, even as the last resort, are but mere duty and obligation, then every good deed, in the deepest sense of the metaphysics of morals, may appear, if so one wishes, as a particular case, in which the fulfilment of a disappearing obligation does not of course come to an end through the one action, but continues as long as the reason for the latter persists. Accordingly, the aid given to anybody would be the ratio cognoscendi [34] that here extends an ideal line of duty from man to man and reveals the timelessness of its perpetuation, once the bond has been achieved.

The poor have a **right** to relief, and there is also an **obligation** to provide relief that is not directed to the poor as people entitled to it, but to society which demands it from its bodies and certain groups for its self-preservation. Beside these two forms of the right-obligation relationship, there is now a third which more or less holds sway over moral consciousness. The general public and the well-to-do have the obligation to assist the poor; this obligation finds its sufficient end in the improved situation of the poor. A claim from the latter corresponds to it, as the other side of the purely moral relation between the needy and the well-to-do. If I am not mistaken, the emphasis within this relation has somewhat shifted since the eighteenth century. The ideal of humanity and of the rights of man, particularly in England, twisted the centralizing standpoint inherent in the Elizabethan poor law, according to

22

which work had to be provided for the poor in the interest of the collectivity. Instead, each poor person, no matter whether he was able to work but did not want to, was entitled to a living minimum.[35] By contrast, modern charity lays stress on the moral obligation of the donor, in the correlation between it and the moral right of the recipient. Obviously, this form will be complicated in reality by the presence of private charity as distinct from State charity, and its sociological significance under this aspect still needs to be addressed.[36]

For a start, one needs to substantiate the already outlined tendency to treat poor relief more as the concern of the broadest circle of the State, after originally everywhere it had had its basis in the community. As such, it had been chiefly the consequence of the confraternities that had kep the community together. It had been the most natural thing for the members of the local community to aid the needy among them, before the suprapersonal structure, which the individual saw growing around and on top of him, changed the community into the State. The free movement of people completed the process materially and psychologically. To this one may add what is most important for the sociology of the poor, namely that of all the social claims of a truly general and non-individualistic character, that of the poor is the most affecting. Aside from such emotions that accidents and sexual provocations may arouse, there is nothing more impersonal, more indifferent to the other qualities of their objects, than want and penury, and at the same time, more effective and direct a plea. This has always lent a specifically local character to the obligation towards the poor. To centralize it into such a large circle and to make it visible not directly but only through a general concept of poverty, all this has been one of the longest roads between the immediately perceptible and the abstract, ever trodden by sociological forms.[37] As the change of the provision for the poor into an abstract obligation of the State was completed--in England, in 1834, in Germany, about the middle of the century--its nature too was altered to make it correspond to the centralization. Above all, the State still holds the community responsible for the main part of the welfare of the poor, but only as its agent. The administration at the local level has become a mere device, meant to secure the greatest efficiency. The community is no longer the starting point, but rather the point of transmission in the relief process. Therefore, the welfare associations everywhere will be organized with that end in mind. Thus, for instance, in England, they are organized in such a way as to operate a workhouse,[38] and are deliberately freed in this manner from the one-sidedness of local influences. The growing efforts of the salaried welfare officers go in the same direction. The poor appear to them much more as the representatives of the collectivity on which they depend for their pay, whereas the unpaid social workers, those who function more like **human beings**, so to speak, will prefer the earlier, human, that is man-to-man, perspective to the merely objective stance. Finally, a division of functions is introduced, which is highly significant sociologically. The fact that the relief of the poor is still in essence delegated to the community suits the purpose for that very reason, as each case must be handled individually. This is possible only in close proximity to and through a familiarity

24

with one's environment. Furthermore, if the community is to grant the relief, it must find the means, otherwise it would spend the State funds too freely.[39] Notwithstanding, there are cases of penury as a result of illness, blindness, deaf-mutism, insanity, permanent infirmity that are not put at risk by the operational systematic prearrangement as long as they and the necessary administrative procedure are established on thoroughly objective criteria. In such cases, the social services are more technical, and for that reason, the State or the larger association are more efficient. The greater resources and a centralized administration are a net advantage in cases in which personal circumstances and the local environment matter less. Moreover, alongside of the qualitative determination of the direct services provided by the State, there is the quantitative determination which sets them apart from private charity, in particular. The State or the public in general attend only to the most urgent and immediate needs. Everywhere, and most clearly in England, poor relief is guided by the firm principle that only the minimum necessary for living should be granted from the pockets of the taxpayers.

All this is closely linked to the intellectual actions of the whole collectivity. The community comprises the energies and the interests of many individuals but can accommodate their peculiarities only when the whole organization of its division of labour, in which its members perform different functions, is open to debate. If instead, a uniform treatment is demanded, whether directly or through a representative body, its contents can retain only that minimum of the personal sphere that coincides with everybody else's.[40] It follows first of all that no expenditure on behalf of the collectivity may be larger than what its most frugal member is expected to spend. A close-knit community may give way to a bout of extravagant generosity. Nevertheless, when the will of each individual cannot be known directly, but must be assumed by a commissioner, the estimate can only equal the least that one is willing to surrender. Of course this is not a logically imperious necessity --its opposite is no logical contradiction either-- but the affirmation of a psychological dogma, which by the overwhelming extent of its empirical corroboration, has acquired the practical value of the logically demonstrable. Likewise, mass interaction has by necessity to embrace the lowest degree of the intellectual, economic, cultural, aesthetic, and other scales. The legislation in force is conceived as the ethical minimum; the logic valid for all represents the intellectual minimum; the 'right to work', claimed for all, can only be extended to those who display the minimum of their abilities;[41] the affiliation to a political party demands the acknowledgment in principle of the minimum of its fundamentals, without which the party would not exist.[42] This type of the social minimum finds its full expression in the outright negative character of mass interests and interactions.

EXCURSUS ON THE NEGATIVITY IN PATTERNS OF COLLECTIVE BEHAVIOUR

In many respects, the unity of the phenomena just mentioned is attained only through negations. Actually, they often develop a negative character in direct relation to their numerical

26

size. *In mass actions, individual motivations are often so different that the more their unification becomes a possibility, the more their contents is purely negative, even destructive. The discontent conducive to the great revolutions consistently feeds on a good many sources which frequently are so antagonistic that their coming together for a positive cause would be impossible. Therefore, the development of the latter is the concern of the narrower circles and the result of personal actions taken by individuals representing divergent forces, which when assembled in a mass, would have only an emptying and devastating effect.*[43] *In this sense, one of the greatest historians has come to the conclusion that the crowd is always ungrateful: were the whole to reach a prosperous state, the individual, nonetheless, would above all feel what he still lacks personally. The dismantling of individual decisions, which leaves only the negative to the collectivity (this indeed must be taken with a grain of salt, and besides, is not intended to show by what means society overcomes the fate of its forces), was made very clear by the earlier Russian revolutionarism, for instance. The immense geographical expanse, the cultural differences between individuals, the diversity of pursued goals, all predominant in that movement, have made of the notion of nihilism, of the very destruction of all that exists, the adequate expression of the common trait of all its elements.*

The same trait is made manifest in the results of the great plebiscites which so often and quite incomprehensibly are outright negative. Thus, for instance, in 1900, in Switzerland, a federal law about accident and sickness insurance was rejected just like that by a referendum, after it had been passed unanimously by the representatives of the people in both the National Council and the Council of the States. This, in fact, has been the fate of most of the bills submitted to referenda.[44] To say no is the simplest way out and therefore, the broad masses, the elements of which cannot agree on a positive aim, find themselves united in the rejection. The standpoints from which the different groups individually rejected the law were extremely diverse: particularistic and ultramontane, agrarian and capitalist, technically and politically partisan, so nothing but the negation could hold them together. Certainly, the opposite may happen for the same reason: when many small groups meet anyway in their negative determination, as they intimate or prepare their union. Thus, it has been stressed that the ancient Greeks had in fact shown great cultural differences among themselves. Nonetheless, when one compares the Arcadians and the Athenians with their contemporary Carthaginians or Egyptians, Persians or Thracians, they show a lot of common negative characteristic features. There was no human sacrifice or deliberate mutilation anywhere in historical Greece, nor was there any polygamy, sale of children into slavery or unlimited obedience to a particular person. All the positive differences aside, this commonality of the merely negative enhanced their awareness of belonging to a cultural circle that transcended their particular city-states.

The negative character of the bond that unifies the larger circle becomes evident above all in its norms. The grounds are laid for it by the fact that the binding stipulations of every kind must be simpler and less inclusive, the larger the sphere of their validity, all other things being

28

equal. For a start, one may think of the acceptance of the rules of international courtesy which are by far fewer than those to be observed within every restricted circle.[45] Afterwards, one may turn to the fact that the individual states forming the German Empire have usually shorter constitutions the larger those states are. Hence the principle: as the size of the circle grows, the fewer are the ties of the collectivities that join one another to form a social entity.[46] For that reason, although it may look like a paradox, it is possible by means of a minimum of norms to hold together a larger group more easily than a smaller group. Qualitatively speaking, the larger the circle, the more forbidding and restrictive the character of the patterns of conduct which are demanded of its members in order for the circle to subsist as such. The positive ties between members, that lend to the life of the group its particular contents, must ultimately be left to the discretion of each individual. The diversity of persons, interests and events becomes too great to be controlled from one centre; the latter is still left with the prohibitive function. It states what one should not do under any circumstances,*

---

* That is the reason why an English proverb says: the business of everybody is the business of nobody [*in English in the original text – Ed. note*]. The fact that the action becomes particularly negative as soon as it is turned to the plurality makes clear the reason behind the apathy and the forbearance with which the otherwise energetic North Americans regard public abuses. There, one shuffles it off on to the public opinion to achieve everything. Hence the fatalism of the following sentence: making each individual feel his insignificance disposes him to leave to the multitude the task of setting right what is everyone else's business just as much as his own [*in English in the original text – Ed. note*].

sets the limits of freedom instead of steering it, by which is indeed meant only the course of an evolution permanently frustrated and deflected by other trends. That is what happens wherever a larger number of divergent religious sentiments or interests must combine into an entity. Allah has emerged from the decline of the Arab polytheism, as the universal concept, so to speak, of God. By necessity, polytheism fosters the fragmentation of the circle of the faithful as long as its sections turn to their various deities in their different ways, according to the variety of their spiritual and practical inclinations. For that reason, Allah's abstract and unifying character was negative at first. His original nature was 'to abstain from evil' and not to urge to good acts. He was only 'the restrainer'.[47] The Hebrew God, who brought about or expressed a social and religious concentration, unprecedented in ancient times, against all the divisive polytheisms and the unsocial monisms, such as the Indian, formulated his most urgent command as: thou shalt not. In Germany, the positive life relations, that serve as the basis of civil law, were brought together in the Civil Code only some thirty years after the foundation of the Empire. On the other hand, the Criminal Code, with its prohibitive provisions, had been compiled as early as 1872. What makes the interdiction particularly suited to combine smaller groups into a larger one is the situation that the opposite of interdiction is not always the command, but quite often the permissible. Thus, when in a group A, no α must occur, but β and γ may; in group B, no β, but α and γ, and in group C, no γ, but α and β, and so on. The composite construct, made up of A, B, and C, may be grounded on the interdiction of α, β and

30

γ. The integration, though, is possible only if in A, β and γ are not commanded but only permitted, which means that they may also be refrained from. If instead of this, β and γ are positive commands, as much as α is an interdiction, and likewise in B and C respectively, no union would result, because in that case what is expressedly commanded on one side is interdicted on the other. Here is an example. From time immemorial, every Egyptian had been forbidden to eat a particular species of animals, sacred in his area. The doctrine that sanctified abstention from meat consumption of any kind came into being as the outcome of the political fusion of a number of local cults into a national religion, headed by a uniformly ruling priesthood. The unification could take place only through the synthesis or generalization of all those interdictions. Had the consumption of all the animals previously allowed in each province, and from which one could have also abstained, become mandatory in a positive way of sorts, there would have been no way of bringing together the particular rules in force in each sect, or part, into a broader whole.[48]

The more general a norm that is valid for an ever larger group, the less its observance is meaningful to and characteristic of the individual. On the other hand, its infringement may have extremely severe consequences for the individual, which single him out from the group. It is decidedly so in the intellectual sphere, in particular. Theoretical communication, without which generally speaking human society would not exist, rests on a small number of generally accepted norms, which we describe as logical, indeed, even when we are not aware of them in the abstract. They form the minimum which must be *acknowledged by all those who in general want to communicate with one another. This minimum lies at the basis of the briefest acquiescence between perfect strangers, as well as of the daily coexistence of those close to one another. Conformity to these simplest norms is the most general and persistent condition of all sociological life, even though their representation never coincides with empirical reality. Thus logic cuts through all the variety of inner and outer world views and creates a certain common ground, the abandonment of which every intellectual community, in the broadest sense of the word, must repeal. On a closer look, though, the logic neither implies nor provides any positive hold. It is only a norm, against which one should not trespass. Conformity to it warrants no particular distinction or benefit. All the attempts to gain individual recognition just with the help of logic have failed utterly. For that reason, its sociological significance is as negative as that of the Criminal Code: only its infringement begets odd situations and exposure.[49] Persistence in these norms has no other effect for the individual but to give him the possibility both theoretically and practically to remain in the community. Certainly, the intellectual connection itself may run aground because of a thousand internal divergencies, even when strictly adhering to logic. Nevertheless, by violating logic, the connection must fail to materialize just as the moral-social cohesion may crumble even while in fact all penal interdictions are carefully avoided. But by infringing these norms, it always comes to pieces. Things are not different with the societal norms, in the narrow sense of the term, as far as they are effectively common to a circle. Conformity to*

32

*them is not peculiar to anybody, but their in-
fringement is, and in the highest degree. The
most general norms within a circle only want not
to be transgressed; whereas the special norms
that keep the smaller groups together will bestow
upon their individual members a positive character and distinction, in the measure of their
specialization. The practical advantages of otherwise utterly empty societal forms of politeness
also rest on this relationship. Even if from their
most punctilious observance we need not infer the
real high esteem and loyalty of which they assure
us. Their slightest infringement, on the other
hand, convinces us unmistakingly of the absence
of those feelings. Greeting someone in the street
is no proof of respect. Refraining from doing so
decidedly passes for a lack of respect. These
forms of courtesy are quite useless as symbols of
actual inner inclinations. Nevertheless, they are
quite apt to convey the negative, in the sense that
the slightest omission may radically and definitely
determine one's relation to another person. As a
matter of fact, it acts both ways, as far as the
form of courtesy, wholly general and conventional, is the proper essence of a relatively large
circle.*

*

Thus, the community's response to the poor
is reduced to a minimum, and that is quite consistent with the typical nature of its actions. Its
motive, namely that such an action is certain in its
contents only with regard to each individual, has
still another ground for restraint, namely that the
relief of the poor, reduced as it is to a minimum,
has an **objective** character. It is possible to

33

establish quite accurately what is needed in order to preserve anyone from physical deterioration. Every overstepping of that limit, every attempt to raise its level requires far less univocal criteria, and is left to the discretion of subjective ways and measures of evaluation. I said earlier that the cases best suited to receive State relief are those which subjectively are not very dissimilar, and for that matter do not call for a subjective assessment of indigence, particularly in such circumstances as illness, and physical disability. On the other hand, the individually evaluated cases would better devolve upon the narrower local community. Such an objective determination of necessaries, that may incline the largest collectivity to intervene, is considered seriously only when the relief is reduced to a minimum.[50] The old epistemological correlation between generality and objectivity is here at work once again. In the field of knowledge, true generality, the acceptance of a proposition not as historically accurate but ideally, in virtue of the universality of the mind, is an aspect or an expression of its objectivity. On the other hand, one or many individuals may be certain beyond any doubt of the same proposition which for them carries the full weight of the truth but lacks the special stamp which we precisely call objectivity. In practice, though, one may not in principle expect the collectivity to act unless it has an absolutely objective ground. Whenever the ground for action is considered from a subjective standpoint only, and there is no purely objective confirmation, the claim, although as pressing as its satisfaction is worthy, is addressed only to an individual. The fact that the claim refers to purely individual circumstances demands that it is met by individuals only.

Whenever the objective standpoint goes hand in hand with the tendency to nationalize all the poor relief--which indeed has nowhere been carried out in full until now[51]--the logical application of the normative scale plainly means objectivity not only on the part of the poor but also in the interest of the State. Here the essentially sociological form of the relationship between the individual and the collectivity has its proper effect. Whenever functions and interventions are transferred from individuals to the collectivity, the latter tends to regulate the individual action either too much or too little. Thus with regard to compulsory education, it is demanded that the individual should not learn too little, but it is up to him whether he wants to learn more or 'too much'. With the introduction of the legal work-day, it has been provided that employers should not ask too much from their employees, but it has been left to them to decide how much less. In this way, the regulation affects only one side of the action, while the other is left to the discretion of the individual. That is the outline in which our socially controlled actions appear to us. They are limited at one end only, so to speak. Society sets bounds to their maximum or their minimum, while on the other hand, they are left open to subjective discretion. Nevertheless, this outline may be deceptive at times, since there are cases in which social regulation takes into consideration both ends. It is only the practical interest that concentrates on one end while overlooking the other. Thus, for instance, where the private punishment of a crime has been turned over to society and to the objective criminal law, what as a rule, one takes into consideration is only the prospect of a greater certainty that the retribution will be exacted in a truly satisfactory way. In reality, though, the concern is not only to mete sufficient punishment, but also not to punish excessively. Society protects not only the eventual victim, but also the criminal against the excess of subjective reaction.[52]In other words, society sets as objective measure of punishment that which corresponds to its social interests, and not the desires or the aims of the victim. That occurs not only in circumstances that are legally well established. Every societal stratum, that does not find itself at the bottom, sees to it that its members may afford to spend a certain indispensable minimum on clothing, and establishes a floor on 'proper' dress. Those who cannot break through it no longer belong to that social category. Another limit is set at the other end, but not so trenchant, and not with the same determination: a certain standard of luxury and elegance, and at times even of modernity, may not be fit for this or that circle, and whoever overreaches it would incidentally be treated as not quite belonging. Thus the group does not allow the freedom of the individual to expand fully on this other end, either. Rather it sets objective limits to subjective preferences, that is to say, such limits that are required by supraindividual living conditions.[53] This basic form repeats itself when the collectivity assumes the relief of the poor. While it seems mostly to be interested in setting limits to the relief, so that the poor should receive their right share, that they should not receive too little, there is still another concern, practically less effective, that they should not receive too much. The inadequacy of private charity lies not only in the too little but also in the too much; it inculcates laziness in the poor, makes an economically unproductive use of the available means, and arbitrarily favours some at the expense of others. The subjective impulse to do good sins in both directions, and although the danger of excess is not as great as that of insuffiency, the objective norm that sets a traceable standard derived not from the subject as such but from the interest of the collectivity aims at preventing that excess.

This elevation above the subjective standpoint is as relevant to the benefactor as it is to the recipient. By intervening only where there is a complete absence of means, objectively determined, the English public welfare excludes the evidence of personal merit. It so happens that the workhouse[54] hardly offers an attractive opportunity which only those at the end of their tether are likely to consider.[55] Its complement, for that reason, is the private charity which aims at the specific, deserving individual and can concentrate more on his particular needs, while the State takes care of the most urgent. Private charity has the task to rehabilitate those poor who are already protected against hunger by the State to earn their upkeep again, to heal the distress for which the State can provide only temporary alleviation. It is not the need as such the terminus a quo[56] that characterizes private charity, but rather the ideal of producing self-supporting and economically worthy individuals. The State deals with the causal aspect, whereas private charity is concerned with the teleological. To put it differently, the State comes to the aid of poverty, and private charity to the aid of the poor.

There is here a sociological difference of the first order. Abstract concepts, certain elements of which crystallize in the individually complicated reality, often acquire a vitality and effectiveness in practice, that are seemingly more suitable to whole concrete phenomena. It starts with quite intimate relations. Certain erotical relationships mean no more and no less than that one of the parties at least is not seeking the beloved but love, that is only the emotional value which it alone may experience, often showing a remarkable lack of interest in the personality of the beloved. Likewise, in matters of religion, what at times appears as essential is that a certain kind and degree of religiosity are prevalent while its carriers are irrelevant.[57] The conduct of the priest or the ties of the believers with their community are ruled by this general view, without any concern for the particular motive which induced the mood in the individual. Moreover, no other special interest is taken in those individuals than as agents of the impersonal action, if at all. There is a rationalism which from a social-ethical point of view requires that the traffic between people should be grounded in the subjective authenticity as such. Truth, as objective quality of a statement, should be demanded by everybody to whom the statement is addressed, while remaining fully indifferent to the particular qualifications and circumstances of the case. There can be no special, individually parcelled-out right to truth coming from the latter. It is the truth, and not the eloquence or the reception in their individualization, that is the precondition, the contents or the merit, of the group interaction.[58] Criminologists tend to split on the same issue: is the punishment intended for the crime or for the criminal? When the crime is committed, an abstract objectivism demands punishment in order to offset the disturbed real or ideal order. It

38

demands punishment in virtue of the logic of ethics, as a consequence of the impersonal fact which the crime is. From the other standpoint, only the culpable subject should be made to suffer. The action of punishment is introduced not because the crime happens as something objective, but because a subject through whom the crime has become a concrete act requires expiation, education, and whatever is needed to make him harmless. Thus, when deciding the degree of punishment, all the individual details of the case will have to be taken into consideration as much as the general fact of the crime. This double stance may be applied to poverty as well.

One may start with poverty as an objectively determined phenomenon and seek to do away with it as such. Whoever the poor may be, whatever the causes of their poverty, whatever the individual consequences that always result from it, poverty demands relief, compensation for this social deficiency. On the other hand, one may take an interest in the needy individual, because he is poor, certainly, but by the help given him, the overall poverty will not be reduced proportionally. Rather it is the particular needy man who is helped out. His poverty acts here as an individual and singular destiny, his. It is only the actual inducement, so to speak, to concern oneself with him. He must be brought as a whole person to a situation in which the poverty disappears by itself. That is the reason why social services aim more at the fact of poverty, and the other stance, at its cause. Moreover, it is sociologically important to notice that the social distribution of the two kinds of relief between the State and private persons changes as soon as one follows the causal chain one step farther. The State--in

England most decisively--meets the externally obvious need, while private charity attends to individual causes.[59]Likewise, it is the business of the collectivity alone to develop the fundamental economic and cultural conditions that form the basis of those personal circumstances. It has to develop them in such a way that they should give the least chance to individual feebleness, perilous propensities, incompetence, or bad luck to result in impoverishment.[60]In this as in many other respects, the collectivity, its condition, interests and actions have an overall effect on individual decisiveness. On the one hand, it represents an immediate field that contains the elements of its image, the results of its peculiar existence. On the other, it is the wide subsoil from which individual life grows, but in such a way that from its unity the diversity of individual inclinations and circumstances provides the field of the whole with a great variegation of individual manifestations*.

---

* Perhaps it is worth remarking here, out of context, that the comprehension of the individual gestalt through the social allows itself to assume one form, in the same way in which the root and the fruit combine into a whole. As the individual appears there as a kind of transitional form against the societal being, so does the latter function as mere intermediate stage of individual development. This in turn results from the innate basic substance of the personality which we cannot grasp in its purity, outside the shape given to it by the historical milieu, but only feel as the persistent substance of our personal existence, and as the sum of its possibilities that are never fully exploited. On the other hand, at the end of our existence, as it were, we are confronted with the most extreme, clear and formed phenomenon or complex of phenomena which existence brings in support of the individualistic standpoint. Between the two lie the social influences which we receive, the conditions in which society shapes each of us into the appearance we make, and the whole stop-go which we pass through. Thus by its actions and representations, society provides the stage on both sides of which stands the individual creature. The latter is

The French principle concerning the poor reveals a stark contrast to the English principle which has been the occasion for these generalizations. In France, poor relief has been considered the concern of private associations and persons, as a matter of course, while the State is expected to intervene only when the former are deficient. Such a reversal naturally does not mean that the private sector would attend to the most pressing needs, as does the State in England, and that the State is concerned with what exceeds this minimum and is individually desirable, as is the case of private charity. There is no mistaking it that the French principle in its contents does not draw such a clear and fundamental distinction between the two forms of relief, as the English. In practice, the situation of the poor is often the same in both countries because of that. Nonetheless, a difference of the first order is implicit here from a sociological standpoint, and that is very plain: it is a special case of the more general process by which the direct interaction of the elements of the group changes into the action of the supraindividual, unifying collectivity. Once it happens, it admits of continuous adjustments, replacements, and priority shifts between the two forms of social activity. Whether the social tension, or discord, which make themselves manifest as individual poverty, will be solved directly between the elements of society or by those elements come together into a unity,

the agent of those forces that carry him from one stage to the other and exert pressure on society from all sides, as from another standpoint, the social conditions and events press on the individual. Furthermore, he is the agent that mediates between their common groundwork and their actual manifestations.[6] [1]

whether one or the other, it is obviously a motive of decision which will be demanded with formal similarity from the whole societal sphere, although only seldom as clearly and distinctly as in this case.[62] While making these suggestions, one need not overlook the fact that 'private' charity is very much a social event, a sociological form which assigns to the poor a place as organic link in the life of the group no less decisively, although it may not seem so at a glance. This fact is brought out in sharp relief by the forms of transition between the two: on the one hand, the poor tax, and on the other, the legal obligation of sustenance towards poor relatives. As long as a special poor tax is in force, the relationship between the collectivity and the poor does not yet attain that abstract purity which places the poor in direct unity. The State is more likely the go-between which channels the individual contributions, that are no longer voluntary, to their destination. As soon as the poor tax merges with the general tax obligation and the community revenues, that relationship between the poor and the collectivity is completed. Poor relief becomes a function of the collectivity as such, and no longer of the sum of individuals, as in the case of the poor tax. Common interests make capital, so to speak, in a still more specialized form, out of the relief extorted by law from the needy relatives. Private charity, which as in every other case is part of the structure and the teleology of the collective life, is here dominated by the latter, as a result of its intentional deterioration.[63]

It has been said above that the relationship between the collectivity and its poor is a constructive function of society as formal as the relationship between the collectivity and its civil servants or its tax-payers. Now I intend to examine this assertion once more, this time from the standpoint just reached. Earlier, I have likened the poor to strangers, as they similarly stand **away** from the group. Nevertheless, the confrontation implies a most definite **relation** that draws them into the life of the group as one of its elements. Certainly, in this way, the poor stand **outside** the group to the extent they are mere objects of the activity of the latter. Notwithstanding, this marginality is, to put it briefly, only a special form of participation.[64] In society, all this finds itself in a relationship similar to that between spatial separateness and consciousness, to use Kantian terms. Although in space everything is separate, and the subject too, as observer, is external to the other things, the space itself is 'in me', in the subject considered in the broader sense. At a closer look, the double position of the poor, like that of the strangers, may in general be noticed in all the elements of the group, though in varying degrees. However much an individual may contribute to the life of the group with positive effects, however intimately he may blend the contents of his personal life with that of the circle and let it **unravel** in the swirl, at the same time he still **faces** the collectivity, whether it takes him or leaves him, whether it treats him well or badly, whether he is deeply or only shallowly committed to it. In short, whether as party or object of the social circle, he still belongs to the social circle, as subject facing it, as link, as subject-part, in virtue of those very actions and positions that confirm those relations. The duplicity of the position, which logically is very difficult to explain, is but an elementary sociological fact. This has been made clear in another context, in

43

connection with such a primary structure as marriage. Each of the spouses regards the marriage under certain circumstances as a free-standing structure, so to speak, apart from either, causing obligations, expectations, good things and bad. This is not seen as coming from the other spouse as a person, but rather from the whole that makes an object of each of its parts, despite the fact that the whole itself consists of these parts only. This relationship of the simultaneously internal and external positions becomes even more apparent and complicated as the number of links in the group increases. Not only because the whole assumes an autonomy which overpowers the individual, but above all, because the most decisive differentiations have at their disposal an entire gamut of nuances in that double relationship. In order to turn them into an object, to 'deal' with them so as to subdue them, or recognize them as a force to be reckoned with, the group applies particular standards that are in turn specific respectively to the prince, the banker, the socialite, the priest, the artist, and the civil servant. On the other hand, the group draws them in as direct elements of its life, as part of the whole which then again confronts other elements. This is perhaps quite a unitary attitude of social reality as such, which manifests itself separately under the two aspects, or appears so different from the two distinct standpoints. It is roughly like the separate representation of the soul, which is contrary to it, and so far from it, as to be entirely free from it, and so may be influenced by the mood of the whole: coloured, heightened or toned down, shaped or dissolved, while at the same time it is still an integrating part of this whole, an element of the soul which

44

consists only of the combination and integration of such elements.[65] The poor assume an unequivocal position in that range of relations with the collectivity. The relief to which the collectivity is bound by special interests but which the poor in most cases have not the right to claim, turns them into an object of the group action, places them at a distance from the whole, makes them often live as corpus vile[66] on its charity, and as often because of this, turns them into embittered enemies of the whole. The State makes it explicit when it debars the recipients of public alms from enjoying certain civic rights. Nevertheless, this marginalization[67] is no absolute severance. Rather it is a firm tie with the whole, an element without which the whole would be different from what it is. Through this connection, obtained accordingly, the poor enter the network of the totality, no matter whether it sets them apart or treats them as objects.

These propositions, though, do not seem to apply to the poor in general, but only to a certain section, namely those who receive relief, while there are quite a lot of poor people who receive none. The existence of the latter points to the relative character of the notion of poverty. Poor is everyone whose means do not suffice to achieve his end. This purely individualistic notion may be pared down for practical purposes to those ends which may be considered worth attending to, independently of any arbitrary and merely personal considerations. First of all, those imposed on the human being by nature: food, clothing, shelter. Only one cannot with any certainty establish a level of those needs that is valid in all circumstances, and below which there is absolute poverty.[68] Moreover, every milieu, in general,

45

and every social category, in particular, have typical needs, and the inability to satisfy them means but poverty. Hence the fact, which seems banal in developed cultures, that persons who are poor within their class would no longer be poor in the class below, if with their means they were able to meet the typical ends of that class. At the same time, and in absolute terms, the poorest member of a class may not suffer from the discrepancy between his means and his class-determined needs, and so, psychologically, poverty does not exist for him. On the other hand, the wealthiest man may set himself goals loftier than the aspirations of his class and beyond his means, and as a result, also psychologically, he considers himself poor. Thus individual poverty--the insufficiency of means for a person's ends--may be absent there where poverty assumes a social dimension.[69] On the other hand, it may be present there where there is no mention of poverty in the latter sense.[70] Its relativity has nothing to do with the relation of the individual means to the actual individual ends, which is something absolute, independent in its intrinsic meaning of all that may lie beyond the individual. Rather, it refers to his status-determined ends, to his social a priori which differs from one status to another. Besides, the **level** of needs that each group decides, as it were, to consider the zero point which divides poverty from wealth is a characteristic social-historical distinction. There is always some leeway, and often quite a considerable one, when it comes to draw the line, in conditions that have attained a certain degree of development. There are obviously far-reaching sociological variations concerning, for instance, whether the position of the zero-line reflects the

46

average, whether one needs to belong to the most favoured minority in order not to pass for a poor man, whether on the contrary, a class sets the floor very low, out of a practical instinct, in order to prevent the feeling of poverty from getting out of control; whether an individual presence may be in the position to shift the line (as, for example, when a well-to-do personality settles in a small town or moves into another narrow circle), or whether the group persists in clinging to the once set threshold separating the wealthy from the poor. As poverty is apparent in each social class which has worked out a standard of anticipated needs for each individual, it follows from it, just like that, that in many ways poverty is not eligible for relief.[71] Nonetheless, the principle of relief reaches farther than its official aspect allows it to appear. When, for instance, within an extensive family, the poorer and the wealthier members exchange gifts, the latter profit by this opportunity to give in return to the former something more valuable than what they receive, and in that way, their gifts assume the character of relief: the poorer relatives are given useful objects, that is such objects that make it easier for them to uphold the standards of their class. That is the reason why, when looked at from a sociological standpoint, gifts turn out to be different in different social classes. The sociology of the gift coincides in part with that of poverty. A wide range of reciprocal relations between people may be inferred from gifts: their contents, the intentions behind them, the manner in which the gifts are given as much as the manner of their acceptance. Gift, theft, and exchange are the external forms of interaction, directly linked to the question of property, and from them, each absorbs an immense spiritual wealth, the peculiarities of which in turn mark the sociological course of events. They correspond to three motives of action: altruism, selfishness, and objective norms.[72] The essence of exchange lies in the substitution of a value with another, objectively equal, whereas the subjective factors of goodness or of greed remain outside the action. In the pure concept of exchange, the value of the object is not determined by the desires of the individual but rather by the value of the other object. Of the three, the gift displays the broadest range of sociological connections, as in itself it combines the intention and the situation of the giver and the position of the recipient, with all their individual nuances, in the most varied ways. On the other hand, of the many categories which make possible a so-called systematic ordering of these phenomena, the most important for the problem of poverty seems to be the following alternatives: whether the individual meaning and purpose of the gift lie in the attained end-situation, namely that the recipient should have a certain object of value, or in the very action, the gift being the expression of the giver's intention, of a self-sacrificing love or of a self-aggrandizement that more or less intentionally is projected into the gift. In the latter case, in which the action of giving is its own end-product, so to speak, the question of wealth or poverty obviously plays no role, save under the practical aspect of affordability. Nevertheless, when giving to the poor, the stress does not lay on the action but on the result. The poor must get something. Between them, these two extremes of the category of gift give rise to countless combinations of varying intensities. The more clearly preponderant

48

the latter is, the less possible it often becomes to give to the poor what they want as a gift, because the remaining sociological relations between the persons involved are incongruous with the action of giving. Gifts may always be made, no matter whether considerable social differences are implied, or a great personal intimacy, although it becomes more difficult as the social difference decreases and distance replaces intimacy in personal relations. In the upper classes, one often comes across the tragic situation in which those in distress would willingly accept aid while the well-to-do would as willingly proffer it, yet neither dare to ask or propose. The higher the class, the more that economic a priori, on the other side of which poverty begins, is so laid that poverty is likely to occur very seldom, and of course theoretically it is excluded.[73]Thus the acceptance of aid disqualifies the recipient for the status, and supplies the clear evidence that he is formally removed from his social class. Until this happens, class prejudice is strong enough to render poverty invisible, so to speak, as long as it remains an individual affliction and does not assume any social dimenions. Among the assumptions on which the life of the upper classes rests is that anybody individually may be poor, in other words, he may remain within his class even if his means are below the needs of the class, without for that reason to be obliged to reach out for aid. That is why he is poor in the social meaning of the word[74] only as soon as he is aided. From a sociological perspective, it is generally correct to say that poverty does not come first to be followed by relief: this again is much more the fate of the individual form.[75] Rather everybody who benefits from relief or should benefit from it, given his sociological circumstances, is called poor, even if he happens to be left out.

The social-democratic statement that the modern proletarian is quite poor but not a pauper is meant wholly in this sense. The poor as a sociological category are not the result of a certain degree of deficiency and privation, but because they receive relief or they should do so, in keeping with the social norms. Accordingly, poverty is not strictly speaking to be defined as a condition that is quantiatively determinable, but only in keeping with the social reaction that sets in a certain situation, just like crime, which is so difficult to conceptualize directly, and has been defined as 'an action on which public punishment is inflicted'. So too, nowadays, some people do no longer determine the essence of morality by taking into consideration the inner state of the subject, but rather from the result of his action. His subjective intention counts in so far it normally yields a certain socially utilitarian result. Likewise, many a time, the notion of personality is no longer defined as a firmness of character that is directed outwards and qualifies the individual for a certain social role, but the other way round. The elements of society that play a certain role in it are called personalities. The individual condition with its extruding nature has no longer the pride of place in the concept. It has been substituted by social teleology. What is individual is established by the manner in which the surrounding collectivity treats it as a result. Wherever this occurs, it is a continuation of the modern idealism which does not try to define things by an essence inherent in them, but seeks to determine them by the reactions which they arouse in the subject. The poor fulfil the function of a link within the ongoing society not because they are poor, but only to the extent society--the collectivity or separate individuals--reacts to them through aid. It is only in the latter condition that they play their particular social role.

First of all, the social notion of 'poor', as distinct from the individual meaning, is what squeezes the poor into society, as a kind of station or connecting rung. As already said, the fact alone that someone is poor does not relegate him to a certain social category of the poor. He is just a poor shopkeeper, artist, employee, and so on, and remains so in virtue of the quality of his activity, trade or position. Inside his social category, he may assume a gradually modified standing on account of his poverty. Nonetheless, individuals of various standings and positions, who find themselves in this condition, do not in any way join a particular sociological unit outside the boundaries of their original class. They swell the ranks of a circle that is characterized by poverty from the moment they receive relief. In many ways, sooner, when the whole constellation would normally call for it, although they are not granted the relief. Certainly, such a group is not held together by the interaction between its members but by the collective attitude which society adopts towards them. Notwithstanding, a spontaneous association of the poor has not always been absent.Thus, for instance, in the fourteenth century there was a Poorman's Guild[76] at Norwich, while in Germany, there were the so-called Brotherhoods of Pilgrims.[77] Somewhat later, in the Italian cities, one comes across a party of the rich, the optimates, as they called themselves. The only criterion for inclusion was the actual wealth of its members. A similar association of the poor would be impossible because of the growing differentiation of society. Individual dissimilarities of background in matters of overall education and convictions, interests and the past are still too wide and persistent to leave to any such community the energy to come together in a genuine association.

It is only in those cases in which poverty brings with it a positive content shared by many that an association of the poor may come into being as such. The most extreme expression of poverty--the absence of a roof--leaves those at a loss in the big cities to flock together in certain places of shelter. When the first haystacks appear in the fields around Berlin, the homeless, known collectively as the 'Penner', turn up to take advantage of them as convenient night encampment in the hay. To be sure, some attempt at organization may occur among them whenever the Penner of each ward have an overseer of sorts, the 'Oberpenner', who allots to the members of the band their places for the night and arbitrates their quarrels. The Penner see to it that no criminal infiltrates their group, and if that happens, they dennounce him to the police to which they often render all kinds of services. Their overseers are well-known characters whom the authorities always know where to find when they need details about some shady individual. Such specific traits of poverty, which reach their extreme in the lack of shelter, are needed nowadays in order to gain momentum for association. In rest, one may notice that the growing general affluence, a more scrupulous police watch, and above all, the social consciousness with its odd mixture of good and bad susceptibilities that 'cannot tolerate' the sight of poverty--all these increasingly impress on

52

poverty the tendency to hide. And this tendency, understandably, isolates the poor from each other even more, and increasingly prevents them from regarding themselves as a cohesive social class, as it would have been the case in the Middle Ages. The class of the poor, particularly in the modern society, is a highly idiosyncratic synthesis. It is the common terminus of the most diverse destinies, to which flow people from the whole gamut of social ranks. No change, no development, no polarization or decline in the life of society go past without depositing their residue in the layer of poverty as in an artificial lake. The horror of this poverty--apart from merely being poor, which is something that each person comes to terms with, and is only a tinge on his otherwise individually qualified position--is the fact that there are human beings who by their social position are nothing else but poor. This incidentally will facilitate an expansive and indiscriminate alms-giving as it happened quite decidedly and clearly in the Christian Middle Ages, and under the rule of the Koran. As long as one accepted it as an official and irrevocable fact, it did not have the bitterness, and in particular, the inconsistency with which the progressive and activist trends of modern times affect a class the unity of which is based on a purely passive reason, namely that society relates to it and treats it in a particular way. There is no clearer evidence that the poor are nothing but poor than whenever the recipients of alms are deprived of political rights. This lack of a positive qualification of one's own has as a result what has already been said above, namely that despite the similarity of their condition, the layer of the poor does not develop any sociologically unifying forces within it on its own. Thus poverty presents quite a peculiar pattern of sociological relations: a number of individuals assumes a wholly specific and organic part in society through their strictly personal destinies. Hence it is not personal want that makes one poor. Rather, people become poor in sociological terms first and foremost when the want is relieved.

NOTES

1. Throughout Simmel's essay, the term 'sociological' refers to a particular perspective, namely of the interaction between the group and the individual, either as member of the former or as an autonomous actor, from the standpoint of the group, the social as opposed to the individual.
2. Latin scholastic phrase literally meaning 'end from which,' that is, starting point.
3. Latin scholastic phrase literally meaning 'end to which,' in other words, goal.
4. 'Soul' (*Seele*) is a term which Simmel uses in more than one way: here, for instance, it approximates what otherwise might be called 'conscience.' The term is used once more towards the end of the essay, on page 44, in an elusive manner. There, it designates a spiritual yet self-sufficient force, closer to Rudolph Otto's numen. It has often been translated into English by such words as 'psyche' or even 'mind,' either term implying a distinction between the physical and the mental, mind and body, which Simmel dismisses.
5. It is left to various social workers to decide, after means-testing those who approach them.
6. See, for instance, Genesis 43.
7. In other words, it is considered in relation to a particular design or purpose of the collectivity or society beyond the want satisfaction of the needy.
8. That is reinforced by the relative isolation of the needy individuals in the industrial urban world and by the hostility, overt or covert, felt for them in a success-worshipping society.
9. This point is resumed and expanded further on page 16.
10. An effect eloquently commented on by George Orwell, among others, in his book, DOWN AND OUT IN PARIS AND LONDON, New York, 1933, page 182ff.
11. This was also the purpose of the means-tested welfare assistance for families with dependent children provided in the American Social Security Act of 1935.
12. As the 1996 reform of the American social welfare has shown.
13. That was also what President Roosevelt meant by 'the freedom from want,' in his 1941 Message to Congress. It is further experienced, in practical life, as the various, more or less subtle ways in which those in need are discouraged to apply for aid.

14.   Shortages of personnel, equipment, facilities and con-
sumer goods, as well as cash have forced the various
equalitarian-totalitarian regimes to settle for a minimum, above which social services are dispensed as
perks or rewards that go with certain offices, and no
other, thus perpetuating the division between haves
and have-nots.

15.   This trend, which reached a climax in Europe in the
first half of the last century, is nowadays 'globalized'
by means of unenforceable universal rights, which by
their vacuous arbitariness, render conscious self-sacrifice absurd. Unsalaried or little-paid activism
offers the highly strung an outlet for their thwarted
egos as much as others work on their own senses
with drugs and alternative external means in order to
chase away such feelings of helplessness and futil-
ity that might assail them.

16.   Nowadays, administrative standardization makes it
easier to righten wrongs when social services meant
for everybody, irrespective of income, are at stake.
On the other hand, in the case of the poor, their
formally granted legal right to contest doubtful or
outright unfavourable decisions remains a dead letter,
a mere closing formula for letters of notification. The
many obstacles that are placed in their way, ranging
from denial of pertinent ground information on which
the particular decision had been taken to the absence
of the free services of a trial lawyer unbiased in
favour of those who pay for them, discourage most
of the poor from seeking the enforcement of their
ever altered rights.

17.   Whether inspired by the Bible or not, the US legisla-
tors have come with a different solution, easier to
implement because of the general tax in force: losses
from thefts and fires up to a certain amount may be
claimed by the victims on their annual tax returns.

18.   The country-wide campaign to salvage family integrity
and values, that has been going on in the US for most
of the decade, makes sense only on such lines: to
reduce the State burden for the maintenance of children with one parent only. It was meant to create a
favourable atmosphere for the introduction of the 1996
changes in the social security regulations.

19.   The reference is to the first draft of the German Civil
Code that was ultimately finalized and published in
1900. More recently, enforceable moral obligations of
maintenance have been restricted to parents of minor
children only. This applies wherever a comprehensive
welfare system is in place and family ties have

56

loosened.

20. Simmel makes this association in his 'Exkurs über dem Fremden', which is part of chapter nine of his SOZIOLOGIE. As 'The Stranger,' it was published in Kurt H. Wolff's selection in English translation, THE SOCIOLOGY OF GEORG SIMMEL, New York, 1950, pp. 402-408.

21. That is, the circle in which the events take place. With regard to the poor, one often talks of such objectives as 'reintegration', insertion, while the French have added 'relaunching' (*rélancement*), as if they have been uprooted and cast away, and what is needed is to bring them back in society. But the poor have never left it, even if they are so marginalized as the homeless who are likely to be ignored by many charities which prefer to deal with the 'working poor.' It is still interaction with them, whatever one may say and not do. A similar wilful exclusion has been tried on the Serbs in Yugoslavia who need to be brought into Europe as if the Balkan Peninsula, where their country is situated, has not always been part of Europe.

22. Out of which 'fund-raising' has developed.

23. In passing, one may say that monasteries also tended to regularize their interaction with their own poor re-leaving them of the stigma of beggary and integrating them in their economies. On the other hand, the system could hardly be protected against rulers and magnates who had no qualms to treat them as reserve banks and confiscate their assets when they themselves were financially in dire straits.

24. I hope that Simmel is here referring to the boards of elected guardians, which were virtually farmers' associations confronted with the same economic problems as the parish, the most important of which continued to be surplus labour.

25. In Latin in the original text. For the explanation of the terms see notes 2 and 3 above.

26. That is the motive of the 1871 law.

27. This is perhaps the principal dilemma of the current ethos of globalization with its inherent marginalization: what to do with displaced populations, economic migrants, asylum-seekers, the socially undesirable, the unemployable disabled, particularly in the conditions of a demographic explosion outside Europe, that turns humanity into a pest.

28. Here Simmel talks about habit-formation, yet his examples are heterologous: his 'do gooder' in the first case bestows gifts on the object of his attention to reinforce in the other qualities which he has detected in

him and which he admires. In this way, he also assumes part of those qualities as a reflection, or as a
return for his investment. On the other hand, in the
second case, he overlooks the very essence of alms,
which in an urban environment, are occasional, unor-
ganized and minimal when left to the passers-by who
act as their conscience and purse allow them. Regularity and uniformity of amount change the alms into an
allowance, a rent, which the beggar interprets as
such. The object of interaction does indeed change the
relationship between the donor and the recipient
because by its form it enhances the latter's status. He
ceases to consider himself a beggar as long as he
receives an allowance. Its abrupt withdrawal, without
the benefit of an explanation shatters all his illusions
and brings him back to the cold reality of his beggary.
He takes it as a bad joke, and considers himself the
object of a mockery which he has done nothing to
provoke. By contrast, the indifference shown by the
abstemious passer-by is preferable because of its clear,
unequivocal message. Beggars do not expect to be given
alms by everybody: were it the case, beggary would not
exist. In ordinary circumstances, a vocal professional
beggar would take his revenge on the parsimonious
passer-by by a show of magnanimity on his part: he
would bless the non-giver all the same, but only to
embarrass him and make him see the meanness of his
own conduct.

29. The distress is more likely to come from the severance
proper, as the giver ceases to be the significant other
for the recipient whose interest in him, the giver,
remained restricted to the financial assistance which he
made available. The cash nexus is the great deperson-
alizer, which destroys any other bonds when it is in-
sinuated among them. Any money transaction frees
the participants of any kind of affection for and moral
obligation to one another beyond the observation of the
conditions for the handling of the money, agreed in
advance. The secrecy of the Talmudic charity in which
both donors and recipients remained secret so not to
shame anyone reflected the awareness of those negative
implications.

30. Latin phrase which may be translated as 'to hate the
person whom one has harmed.'

31. Contrary to any presupposition, this French saying is of
a relatively recent date. It first appeared in print in
1808 in MAXIMES ET PRÉCEPTES DU DUC DE LÉVIS.
At the time, it was rather a reminder to the new nobility that their position was less a confirmation of their

advantages as it was the source of their moral obligations and responsibilities. For Simmel, though, the
phrase acquires a thoroughly ethical content, what may
be summarily described as the nobility of soul, of
character. In other words, it is the assembly of
virtues that prompts their possessor to do good. See
also 'Exkurs über dem Adel' in chapter ten of his
SOZIOLOGIE. An English translation is included in the
volume GEORG SIMMEL: SOCIOLOGIST AND EURO-
PEAN, ed. P.A. Lawrence, New York, 1976, pp.
199-213.
32. Latin phrase meaning a deed performed beyond what
duty requires.
33. Which conveys the regularity of occurence of a
specific event or feature in a population. On the other
hand, what Simmel farther calls 'moral instinct' looks
more like a sublimation of the feudal ethos of
obligation.
34. Latin phrase meaning 'that in virtue of which knowledge of something is possible.'
35. It is interesting to know that this principle reappeared in the aftermath of WWII, in the Universal
Declaration of Human Rights, Articles 3 and 22. The
right to a living minimum was included in the 1989
charter of the European Union, from which Britain
abstained. During the French Revolution that minimum had been expected to be secured by the State
without delay to everybody whose taxes amounted to
less than the wages for one day's work. In keeping
with their 1946 Constitutiom, however, the French
have introduced a law which links the right to a
living minimum to gainful employment which itself is
no longer considered an obligation but a privilege.
F.D. Roosevelt himself had been talking as early as
1941 of a system in which persons **deserving** gainful
employment may obtain it.
36. In the United States the situation is made even more
complicated by the differences in policy from state to
state and even from county to county, compounded by
their and the federal government's tendency to con-
tract out their public services to private, for profit or
non-profit charitable and welfare organizations. Moreover, there are all sorts of semantic differences in
various classifications. Charity is transformed into
social services, while for purposes of taxation, the
government considers tax-exempt institutions as well
as not-for-profit organizations as charities: so a re-
search institute, for instance, is a charity! In real life,
one comes across another differentiation, between phil-

anthropies and charities. The former are those organizations that do not pay taxes on their income
which they use selectively to finance various cultural
and scientific projects, and only indirectly and on a
limited scale, certain charitable organizations meant to
help the needy.

37. 'Form' is a term extensively used by Simmel with a
variety of meanings. Here, as 'sociological form,' it
refers to an abstraction, the formation of a theoretical
concept out of accumulated concrete life experiences,
that in turn can be used to work out rules and regulations meaningfully related to it at societal level.

38. In English in the original text.

39. Fund-raising has appeared as a consequence. The
expansion of social services has turned it into a highly
regarded and well-paid profession. On the other hand,
tax-evasion has been decriminalized on condition that
the moneys are used to finance non-profit projects of
one's choice which the government is less likely to
finance. To them, one may add the individual donations in goods and cash to various charities, in the
fiscal sense, that can be deducted from taxes to a
degree, which also gives the tax-payer the feel-good
opportunity at no extra cost.

40. This has been the principle behind the State-run
welfare system, set up in the Soviet Union and its
satellites, in the aftermath of the wanton destruction
of their material wealth.

41. The claim for cultural diversity is a reaction to the
reductionist uniformization associated with the implementation of the socially acceptable minimum as the
exclusive standard of equalitarian democracy.

42. It has also made Islam, with its few requirements
(the Pillars of Faith), so attractive world-wide to
those on the look out for a satisfactory outlet for their
religious needs. In the twentieth century, on the other
hand, it made possible the creation of mass movements
which superseded the political parties of the previous
century.

43. This is Simmel's argument against the doctrine of the
role of the masses in history, advocated by historical
materialism.

44. The institution is as strong a hundred years later, and
among other things, is what has kept Switzerland out
of the European Union. It has been embedded in the
folk wisdom of the cantons, in the widely circulated
saying: 'The referendum is our right to say No when
Berne has said Yes.'

45. Since Simmel wrote this essay, courtesy in

international relations, already at a low ebb, has been
battered to death in the name of the self-righteousness
of the louder and the stronger.

46. The principle has been at work as far as the US Constitution is concerned. It has remained the longest-
lasting written constitution in the modern world. In
passing, one may also remark that it was adopted
eleven years after the Declaration of Independence,
and that the Bill of Rights was appended to it only
four years later, in 1791.

47. See The Koran 24.21.

48. Here Simmel refers to the logic of obligation or
deontic logic, the main principle of which is that
nothing may be compulsory which is forbidden at
the same time. The logic of the permissible and
the compulsory had been part of moral theology
since early times. Whether it was resorted to however by the Egyptian ruling priesthood in the
consolidation of their authority is still a moot point.

49. Which is exactly what many arsonists and destroyers
of cultural monuments in the twentieth century have
tried to achieve by their acts of vandalism.

50. Generalized in the industrial Western countries to the
whole welfare system, the principle is not new, nonetheless. There, it has already been a working principle since the fifteenth century.

51. Ten years after Simmel wrote the essay, that happened in Soviet Russia which became a test case.

52. Amendment VIII to the US Constitution reflects that
tendency, characteristic of a certain kind of liberalism which acknowledges equilibrium as a vital
structural principle. In periods of 'transition', on
the other hand, independent judges and juries may
ignore those very limitations in their determination
to reform society.

53. In his 1911 essay 'Philosophie der Mode' (The
Philosophy of Fashion), ET published in SIMMEL ON
CULTURE, eds. D. Frisby and M. Featherstone, London, 1997, pp. 187-206, Simmel shows what happens
when individuals and social groups demand continuous
change. As the speed of their development gives them
the edge over the others, the lower groups become
better at imitating the upper strata which in turn
tend to cast away a fashion the moment it is adopted
by a lower group. As the changes in fashion gather
speed, the greater the demand for affordable products
of its kind by all the social groups: the upper, in
order to resist the pressure exerted by their imita-
tors, and the lower, in their quest of objects that at

least should bear the outer semblance of fashion. This, indeed, does not apply to clothing alone, but also to gadgets and lifestyles: think only of the various 'generations' of cellular telephones!

54. In English in the original text.

55. It was only WWII, with its mobilization of all home resources, that put an end to workhouses in Britain, long known as unproductive and demoralizing institutions.

56. Latin for 'starting point.' See note 3 above.

57. In English in the original text.

58. What Simmel points to here is the difference between the collective affirmation of a concept, the achievement of a suprapersonal end which as such requires only a shared conformity to a norm, in this case, religiosity, on the one hand, and on the other, subjective authenticity which is the precondition of communication, and so of individual interaction. That is also to say that suprapersonal cohesion has nothing to do with empirical truth, because objective knowledge is not subservient to social arrangements and does not discriminate between members and non-members of the group, yet without it one could not arrive at the common notion.

59. The division of labour between the two sectors has survived, although the State, directly or through local councils, has considerably expanded the ranges of services considered vital.

60. It is this stance that justifies calling Simmel a social liberal. What one may retain from it, and social workers are fully aware of that, is that it may be socially more difficult to rehabilitate people who have fallen into destitution than to prevent their reaching that stage.

61. Simmel's note has been omitted from Claire Jacobson's translation because of its highly metaphorical and abstract language, which she thought was beyond the understanding of the average social scientist. Actually, it is a pithy definition of the life–long relationship between the individual and society, given by the philosopher that Simmel was. With regard to the pauper, the message which may be derived from it is simply that the way the latter is regarded by the collectivity has a capital effect on his chances of rehabilitation, both moral and material.

62. In the last forty years or even longer, this perspective has broadened to become universal in the aftermath of decolonization. Local issues are met with suprastatal solutions, and consequently with little

success, as long as the will for a unifying global community is missing. The real question now'adays is whether by treating them as an interaction between rich and poor, haves and have-nots, international relations have not been undermined past redress.

63. Private charities have increasingly been run as service businesses, which by paying their staffers fair market salaries and offering them other material benefits, absorb the surplus of man- and brain-power churned out by generalized secondary and higher education. Professor W.W. Rostow's complaint about the lack of coordination among the many organizations in Austin, Texas, where each are addressing only one aspect of the condition of the poor in the town while remaining unconcerned about the others, prevention of impoverishment included, unintentionally confirms the evolution, which is not peculiar to Austin alone. See his book THE GREAT POPULATION SPIKE AND AFTER, New York, 1998.

64. Here Simmel has been using the opposition *Außerhalb* versus *Innerhalb*.

65. See note 4 above.

66. Latin expression literally meaning 'cheap body.' It refers to something which has no other value but as an object of experimentation without regard for outcome.

67. That is, *Außerhalb*.

68. In the year 2000, the World Bank and the United Nations Organization established a threshold for absolute poverty of one US dollar per day for the so-called developing countries.

69. This is a situation very hard to grasp in the United States, in particular, where anarchical individualism and endemic competitiveness of the beggar-thy-neighbour kind are permanent features of social life. When confronted with it in Russia, George F. Kennan named it 'the equality of misery.'

70. As in the 7G countries, a situation which actually places them in a predicament vis-à-vis the developing and the underdeveloped or poor countries, as much as those other countries the economies of which are said to be in transition.

71. This is the case of the considerable number of insolvent households in the United States where it is alleged that some thirty per cent of the families with a monthly income of $60,000 are unable to pay their bills. They may obtain extended repayment periods before they are allowed to declare bankruptcy, but not any other kind of relief before they hit the officially recognized poverty line.

72. This is an approximate translation of Simmel's term *Normierung*.
73. As the main criterion of belonging is not wealth, but another. In the case of nobility, for instance, it is birth.
74. As opposed to the psychological or the economic meanings.
75. ... of poverty.
76. In English in the original text.
77. That is, *Blendengilden*.

POSTFACE

ABOUT THE AUTHOR

*Several years ago, Messrs Routledge of London and New York brought out a hefty three-volume set at the price of $460.00, entitled GEORG SIMMEL: CRITICAL ASSESSMENTS. Mind you, this is not a collection of critical articles by Simmel, but **about** Simmel, and in a large number by English-speaking contemporaries of his; the printed matter by Simmel himself takes only thirty pages in all. It is not a festschrift either, since all the items are mere reprints from other publications. The whole undertaking seems to be yet another perversion in the name of 'scholarship', to bury him under a heavy and expensive slab which that hefty set ultimately is.*

The present publication rallies to those stubborn attempts to allow Simmel to address us over a century spent mostly in annihilating one another, and to make us notice things which we have been overlooking for various reasons and always at our peril. Is it sheer mental lethargy that has discouraged the initiative of publishing a comprehensive English edition of those of his works which he cared about? In this direction, the publication by the University of Massachusetts of a collective translation of Simmel's SCHOPENHAUER AND NIETZSCHE in 1986 is highly commendable, as are Guy Oakes' translations of some of Simmel's essays, mostly epistemological, published by the Free Press and Rowman and Littlefield, respectively. It is a pity, though, that the man who after WWII did most to rekindle the interest in Simmel in the States had to resign himself to the translation and publication of a couple of selections from Simmel's mostly 'sociological' writings. His efforts scored mostly a succès d'estime and did not win him the votes of the American sociologists when he became a candidate for the presidency of their association. I am talking of Kurt H. Wolff.

Until Rudolph H. Weingartner published his doctoral dissertation on Simmel, the philosopher of culture, in 1962, in the United States, the German philosopher had been the domain of the sociologists through a whim of Simmel himself. At a loss for a name for the kind of moral philosophy he was practising, he called it arbitrarily 'sociology', thus disregarding the fact that the term was already deeply entrenched and widely used in the positive sciences to define a certain kind of investigation of social reality, mainly institutional. His dismissive reaction to the objections against his appropriation of that term for his own use: 'it does not matter what you call it' not only cost him a good deal of misunderstanding and even hostility from his contemporaries, and in particular from the practitioners of that science on the Continent and in England, not least among them Emile Durkheim and Max Weber, but also most of the posterity of his philosophical efforts. The academic philosophers refused to see in him but a dilletante with a knack of publicity, or as Georg Lukacs put it, 'an impressionist'. (It was Edmund Husserl who learnt from that mishap, and when the time came to look for a label for his descriptive psychology, chose one from a more distant past when he decided in favour of 'phenomenology', a term hardly used since Hegel.) In America, during his lifetime, Simmel's name and the few American translations of his essays were used to boost and legitimize the discipline of sociology, because Germany was the place from which ideas were imported up to WWI. He was ostracised, though, when at the beginning of that war, for a brief spell, he rallied to the popular enthusiasm. He was readmitted posthumously in 1925, when Nicholas J. Spykman produced a dissertation on Simmel's social theory, in which he tried to isolate those elements which Simmel had derived from experimental psychology, and reuse them in a science of social engineering. Since then Simmel's writings have supplied all kinds of motives for virtuoso displays of academic professionalism on the part of sociologists and philosophers alike. All that, however, could but render his intentions and his achievements more obscure, distant and irrelevant. It is only when one dissociates him from the term 'sociology' and becomes aware of the fact that in his philosophical beginnings, under the influence Eduard Zeller, Simmel started afresh by emulating Socrates, and realizes the continuity, perseverance and consistency in the evolution of his thinking throughout his life, in which the immediate and direct experience remain paramount dimensions of his reflection, that one may be ready to follow him in the journey of discovery.

*

Georg Simmel was born in Berlin on 1 March 1858, the youngest of the seven children of Edward Simmel and Flora née Bodstein. Edward had brought his family from Breslau to Berlin where he had set up a confectionery firm FELIX & SAROTTI which eventually would expand into the famous chocolate factory (still in business), though not under Edward Simmel's control. He died in 1874, when Georg was only sixteen. His only other son, Eugen, had moved to Leipzig where he had become a bookseller and author of a travel book on the Alps, but he too died not long afterwards. As for Georg, he became the ward of Julius Friedländer, a family friend and a musicologist by trade, founder of the music publishing firm EDITION PETERS. His guardian wanted to kindle in him his own passion for music and for hiking in the Alps, and furthermore, financed his university education in the hope that ultimately he would embark upon a university career. So Georg Simmel enrolled as a regular student at Berlin University in 1876, where he began by reading history, then ethnopsychology, and finally, philosophy, while developing an interest in art history and early Italian culture, which would become his secondary specialization and materialize in a thesis on Petrarca. Early in 1881, his dissertation 'Ethnographic and Psychological Inquiries in the Beginnings of Music' (ET 1968) was rejected as inadequate and badly written. At the same time, he was advised instead to develop the ideas from a paper he had written on Immanuel Kant, the eighteenth-century philosopher, which had won Simmel a prize. His new dissertation was accepted in 1883 but an altercation with one of the professors on the commission led to a disciplinary postponement of his trial lectures. It was only in October 1884 that Simmel was granted the accreditation to teach at Berlin University. His inaugural public lectures as privatdocent were delivered in January 1885. For the next fifteen years, despite his own efforts and those of his friends, he remained a privatdocent at Berlin

University, position that brought him no salary but only fees from the students who registered for his seminars and public lectures. He had to supplement his income by writing for the press, and for a while he even tried to churn out verse and prose for the same reason, but quickly realized that he lacked the necessary talent. In 1890, Privatdocent Dr. Georg Simmel married Gertrud Kinel, the daughter of a railway engineer and government official, herself and intellectual and future author of published works on various philosophical questions. It was only in 1898 that the faculty of the Department of Philosophy made a first perfunctory gesture to have Simmel promoted to the next rank in the academic hierarchy, namely of reader, which position excluded the supervision of doctoral dissertations. It presented Simmel's scholarly interests and teaching abilities in a light that only served to feed the prejudices of the Prussian Ministry of Education against him. The fact that as a privatdocent he consistently managed to muster between thirty-five and seventy students for his seminars, and the attendance at his lectures, always held in the University's largest auditorium, surpassed the 150 number increasingly made the University's administration appear incongruous in the eyes of the public. A much attentuated petition to the same Ministry, two years later, finally found a positive response. That was the most the Berlin University and the Prussian Ministry of Education would ever concede to him. It took another fourteen years before he was finally offered a chair at Strassburg University (not a major institution), following the Emperor's positive reaction to a very sober and earnest petition on the part of that University. A further attempt in 1915 to obtain a chair at Heidelberg ended in failure, and when in 1916 Simmel was diagnosed as having an incurable cancer of the liver, he divided the rest of his energies between his professorial duties at Strassburg and the completion of his last major work which was published only posthumously. He died shortly before the French reoccupied the city, closing down the University and expelling its German faculty. He was sixty years old at the time and his friends thought he had been lucky to have done so, and be spared the ordeal of an impecunious old age in a Germany torn by revolutionary turmoil.

Such biographical details largely explain his concern in the lot of those who cannot satisfy their needs by their own means in a prosperous society, which to reiterate, has affluence and stability as its main interests. From the age of sixteen he was cast in the position of supplicant. Although left a legacy by his guardian 'to see him through hard times', those hard times proved to be longer and harsher than it could have been anticipated. He never admitted that he was poor but in his private correspondence with his closest friends. It was in order to put an end to that precarious situation that his younger friend and admirer, Max Weber, intervened, albeit unsuccessfully, to secure him an academic chair. After a delayed accreditation, the world of academia eventually accepted him in its ranks, yet it remained adamant in granting him only the minimum needed to keep him inside the farthest boundaries of its fold throughout, despite consistent evidence of high quality professional performance on his part. To an extent, Simmel was an intruder in academic philosophy. He forced himself upon it, claiming his acceptance on his own terms, of which his indulgence with 'sociology' was the most unfortunate. Moreover, he had no professorial family tradition, and by deciding against ethnomusicology as his profession, a career for which his connection with his musical guardian might have acted as a facilitator, he could expect no indulgence from that sector, either. Socially, he had only himself to rely on to form those connections that would enable him to gain admission to and approval of the intellectual circles of his native Berlin. Nevertheless, acceptance in one circle did not mean automatic access to the others. Thus his participation in the circle round Gustav Schmoller, an economic historian of wide repute and professor at the University who published an early article of Simmel's in his Yearbook, turned to be more of a liability for his university career. Schmoller's views were not to the taste of the officialdom which considered them too socialist. Eventually, as Max Weber had shown, Simmel would not adhere to any of the philosophical chapels either in Berlin or anywhere else. He was more successful in the non-academic cultural world where his extensive publicistic activity may also be regarded as a protracted exchange of gifts between the editors of periodicals and publishers, on one side, and contributors like him, on the other, an expression of their appreciation of his intellect and sensibility. Had he been a wealthy heir as the poet Stefan George, son of a wine merchant, he very likely would have refrained from any contacts with any educational authorities, and instead, remained an independent scholar reflecting in and about the world and writing his books as a result. That the Berlin University kept him at all while discouraging other educational authorities to offer him a better treatment was simply to satisfy its administrators' vanity. By the high attendance his public lectures mustered year in, year out, Simmel provided the University at no additional cost with the means of maintaining its own renown as the most liberal institution of higher education in Germany. Besides, a promotion somewhere else could have been interpreted as Berlin's inability to appreciate him professionally for what he was, a thing it could not allow to happen. To that end all the means were good, anti-Semitic slurs included.

As Simmel's ultimate interests had to do with the meaning of life for the individual who not only exists in but moves through and is also part of a changeable world and cannot be reduced to a bunch of empirical data, his name and his writings continue to be used for ends alien to him, even there where open hostility has been suspended as being 'politically incorrect'. After all, thinking not only hurts but as Simmel's biography shows, it does not pay, either.

S.D.

A NOTE ON SOURCES

For an exhaustive bibliography on charity, welfare, poverty and social work, human rights, aid, and the like, one may easily access the corresponding subject indexes made available by the Library of Congress, for instance. Moreover, almost all the books on those subjects do contain extensive bibliographies of their own. Here are listed only part of those titles which were consulted in the production of the Preface and the Postface, as well as of the notes. They are mentioned here in alphabetical order by author or editor, as the case may be.

Aron, Raymond, *The Imperial Republic*, tr. Frank Jellinek, Englewood Cliffs N.J., 1974. It contains a pertinent discussion of the American foreign aid policy during WWII and after.

Barrat, Claude-François, *La pauvreté*, Paris, 1998, is an economist's approach to poverty in Western Europe and as a subject matter of the United Nations and other international fora.

Blau, Joel, *Illusions of Prosperity: America's Working Families in an Age of Economic Insecurity*, New York, 1999, contains an ample bibliography.

Carr, E.H., *A History of Soviet Russia: The Bolshevik Revolution 1917-1923*, 3 vols., London, 1950, 1952, 1966, is indispensable for all those who want to make sense of the intentions and the achievements in Russia in those years of war communism and of NEP.

Constantelos, Demetrios J., *Byzantine Philanthropy and Social Welfare*, 2nd ed., New Rochelle N.Y., 1991, deals in particular with the ideology which Eastern Christianity developed in the Middle Ages in order to cope with a social plight increasingly perceived to be permanent.

Dion-Loye, Sophie, *Les pauvres et le droit*, Paris, 1997, concentrates on the evolution of the poor law in France, in particular, since the 18th century, and on the more recent influence exerted through the reintroduction of the universal human rights.

Duller, H.J., *Development Technology*, London, 1982, a critical examination of 'growth' and 'development' policies outside the 'developed' world, and the nefarious consequences for the regions where they are applied without regard for the concrete conditions.

Flenley, Ralph, *Modern German History*, London, 1959, useful to get a summary notion of the social and political evolution of Germany in the 19th century and up to WWI.

Fraser, Derek, ed., *The New Poor Law in the*

Nineteenth Century, New York, 1976, a series of articles on various aspects of the social life in Britain, affected by the Reform of 1834 and the subsequent amendments.

Frisby, David and Featherstone, Mike, eds., *Simmel on Culture, Selected Writings*, London, 1997, a large collection of old and new English translations of articles, chapters, and essays by Simmel himself, compiled by two sociologists.

Gaston Ash, Timothy, *A History of the Present*, New York, 1999, presents various developments in the West–East interaction in Europe since the end of the cold war. Gaston Ash himself makes an interesting object of study as a prototype of the 'neo–liberal' intellectual.

Ganz, Herbert, *The War Against the Poor*, New York, 1995, refers to the various ways by which social expenses could and are reduced in the States.

Gassen, Kurt und Landmann, Michael, eds., *Buch des Dankes an Georg Simmel*, Berlin 1958, a festschrift to mark Simmel's centennial. It contains the first systematic bibliography of Simmel's writings by Kurt Gassen, the 1918 article on Simmel by Georg Lukacs, and biographical notes by Michael Landmann, 'Bausteine zur Biographie,' which have served as the source of information for the Postface of the present publication.

George, Vic and Manning Nick, *Socialism, Social Welfare and the Soviet Union*, London, 1980, presents what has been the first nationalized social welfare system in the world.

Gilens, Martin, *Why Americans Hate Welfare*, Chicago, 1999, does explain the relationship between providers and recipients in a country where the right to relief is discouraged in many ways, one of which being its equation with alms–giving. It also contains a copious bibliography.

Goffman, E., *Stigma: Notes on the Management of Spoiled Identity*, New York, 1974, is one of that author's several books examining ways by which disadvantaged people in America deal with themselves in their interaction with those who stigmatize them.

Got'e, Iurii V., *Times of Troubles: Diary of ...*, July 8, *1917 to July 23, 1922*, tr. and ed. Terence Emmons, Princeton N.J., 1988. One of the most interesting testimonies of the events in Moscow and in Russia of that period, written for the drawer by a social historian, living the dismantling of a civilization in no time, so to speak. He was one of the beneficiaries of the ARA generosity.

Grant, Richard and Nijmar Jan, eds., *The Global Crisis in Foreign Aid*, Syracuse N.Y., 1998, is a collection of articles on the subject by various hands, from a variety of positions and of countries.

Harper, Henry Howard, ed., *Letters and Poems of Queen*

Elisabeth (Carmen Sylva), vol. 2, Boston, 1920. The quotation from Secretary of State Hay's note to the American chargé d'affairs in Athens in the Preface comes from this volume, pp. 112-113.

Heisenberg, Werner, *Physics and Beyond*, tr. Arnold J. Pomeranz, New York, 1971. Among other things from his recollections included in this volume, I found quite interesting the description of his experience collecting alms for the Winter Help fund in the streets of Leipzig, as part of Hitler's campaign to cut intellectuals down to size.

Hook, Steven W., ed., *Foreign Aid: Toward the Millenium*, London 1996, a collection of articles, not unlike Grant's quoted above, in which skepticism lies side by side with a stubborn optimism in the campaign of globalization through aid.

Ignatieff, Michael, *The Needs of Strangers*, London 1984, and *Virtual War, Kosovo and Beyond*, New York, 2000, reveal aspects of the administration of international aid in action, so to speak, in his reporting as a journalist in the field.

Kennan, George F., *American Diplomacy 1900-1950*, New York, 1951, a little book made up of a series of lectures delivered at the University of Chicago, is admirable not only for the courage of its author, but also for his going for the essentials and uncovering the constants of America's foreign policy. His *Around the Cragged Hill*, New York, 1993, alongside his other two volumes of *Memoirs*, New York, 1967-1972, and *Russia and the West under Lenin and Stalin*, Boston 1960, shed a lot of light on the relations between Russia and the United States and American diplomacy and participation in the affairs of the world, as they are unravelled by a man with a sense of proportions and of differences.

Levy, Reynold, *Give and Take: A Candid Account of Corporate Philanthropy*, Boston, 1999, shows plainly the difference between philanthropy and charity in America, and moreover, that the former is another venue for public relations and business as such.

Laboriau, Patrick, *Clochard: L'univers d'un groupe de sans-abri parisiens*, Paris, 1993, a French anthropologist who has studied in America, spends some time with a group of homeless, centred on a church in the 15th district. What is annoying is that he never makes any mention of their attitude towards him, what they really thought of him beyond a certain willingness on their part to show him some of the tricks of their trade. But this is the shortcoming of most of such participant-observation studies everywhere.

Lawrence, P.A., ed., *Georg Simmel: Sociologist and European*, New York 1976, another selection of Simmel's articles and essays in English translation.

Leontief, Wassily, *Input-Output Economics*, Fair Lawn N.J., 1966, helpful in understanding the shifts in the thinking behind the cessation of the cold war.

Longmate, Norman, *The Workhouse*, New York, 1974, is a history of that British institution from the end of the 18th century, based on contemporary records, testimonies and public reactions.

Loménie, Louis de, *Baumarchais et son temps*, 2 vols., Paris, 1887 remains one of the most cogent and informed chronicles of the events in which the French factotum involved himself, not least, the organization of the aid to the American colonies.

Mollat, Michel, *The Poor in the Middle Ages*, tr. Arthur Goldhammer, New Haven, 1986. It is interesting for the evolution of the attitude towards the poor in Western Europe, in particular.

Nicolson, Harold, *Peacemaking*, London, 1933. Valuable testimony of the discriminatory treatment to which various countries and their representatives were subjected at the Paris peace conference in 1919, and outside it.

Nove, Alec, An *Economic History of the USSR*, Harmondsworth, 1972; *The Soviet Economy*, 3rd ed., London 1969, and the collection of shorter articles, *Was Stalin Really Necessary?*, London, 1964. By far more understanding of his subject matter than any of the younger Western economic reformers of later Russia, never forgetting the unsurmountable obstacles which nature (not only of the human sort) has raised in her path of development.

Patlagean, Evelyne, *Pauvreté économique et pauvreté sociale à Byzance: 4e–7e siècles*, Paris, 1977, an in-depth and systematic inquiry in the institutions of Byzantium, past the supporting ideology, that uncovers a civilization grounded in poverty. It complements Mollat's study and supplies some answers for Constantelos'.

Polanyi, Karl, *The Great Transformation*, Boston, 1957, c1944, spells out the social problems raised by the development of market economy since the 19th century.

Rose, Michael E., *The English Poor Law 1780-1930*, New York, 1971, a sourcebook of the reforms and the circumstances in which they were carried out, meant as a guide for those interested in the subject matter, and denied access to the Webbs' three-volume history of the English poor law.

Rostow, W.W., *The Great Population Spike and After: Reflections on the 21st Century*, New York, 1998, and *The Stages of Economic Growth: A Non-Communist Manifesto*, New York, 1971, convey the standpoint of the establishment, which enables one to get a better grasp of the American

76

position not only in international relations and economic development but also closer to home, in the conditions of the demographic growth and the shifting distribution of wealth.

Rowe, Michael, *Crossing the Border: Encounters Between Homeless People and Outreach Workers*, Berkeley, 1999, has made me understand the quandary in which social workers find themselves when their own livelihood depends on their carrying out the untenable requisites of particular programs that finance them.

Russell, Bertrand, *The Theory and Practice of Bolshevism*, London, 1920, is the result of a fact-finding mission in Soviet Russia by the British philosopher, intent on contributing to her economic recovery on socialist lines in the aftermath of the war. It aroused Lenin's ire and fed his suspicion of subsequent foreign visitors, however well-intended they confessed to be.

Schapiro, L.B., *The Communist Party of the Soviet Union*, 2nd ed., New York, 1971, interesting particularly for the fact that it deals with the party organization and not with the consequences of its policies upon the country as a whole.

Schiber, Sylvester J. and Shoven, John B., *The Real Deal: The History and Future of Social Security*, New Haven, 1999, has the advantage of bringing together, in one book, the history of the 1935 Social Security Act and its subsequent developments.

Simmel, Georg, *The Conflict in Modern Culture and Other Essays*, tr. and ed. K. Peter Etzkorn, New York, 1968, includes a translation of Simmel's rejected doctoral thesis on ethnomusicology, while *On Individuality and Social Forms*, ed. Donald N. Levine, Chicago 1971, is another selection of short pieces by Simmel in English translation. Both have been preceded by *The Sociology of Georg Simmel*, ed. Kurt H. Wolff, New York 1950, the first solid selection with a corresponding critical apparatus published in the States after WWII. Simmel's *Sociology of Religion*, tr. Curt Rosenthal, New York, 1959, intent to maintain that interest, is useful for grasping not only the notion of the soul but the distinctions between institutionalized religions and individual religious needs and experiences.

Stokke, Olav, ed., *Foreign Aid Towards the Year 2000: Experiences and Challenges*, Portland OR, 1996, interesting for the light it sheds on the Swedish experience in the administration of aid in poor and calamity-stricken regions particularly in Africa and the attitudes emerging from it.

Tocqueville, Alexis de, *Œuvres Complètes, tome XVI, Mélanges*, ed. François Mélonio, includes two memoranda on pauperism (1835, 1837), as well as a letter on pauperism in Normandy by one of the most astute social observer of the

19th century.

Wedel, Janine R., *Collision and Collusion: The Strange Case of Western Aid to Eastern Europe*, New York, 1998, suffers less than other works dealing with the West-East relations from a lack of discrimination in accepting lead-on statements or confessions as fact. It is quite astonishing how many such reporters hardly ever question the intentions of those eager to tell their stories, and in their pursuit of direct contacts turn themselves into willing transmitters of purposefully cut images, as objective truth. Inability to verify the data quells whatever scruples about veracity one might have.

Weingartner, Rudolph, H., *Experience and Culture: The Philosophy of Georg Simmel*, Middletown Conn., 1962, is a readable introduction to the dynamics of Simmel's mental constructs, first presented as a doctoral dissertation in philosophy.

Wells, H.G., *Russia In The Shadows*, New York, 1921, coming one year after Russell's visit there, mentions the first attempts of the West, and of America, in particular, to help rebuild the economy in a country run by what Wells found to be the simplest-minded government in the world, that made virtue out of necessity and put the blame for everything on 'the blocade'.

Wolff, Kurt H., *ed., Georg Simmel, 1858-1918*, Columbus Ohio, 1959, is the American festschrift for Simmel's centennial, which also includes some of his essays in English translation.

Zeller, Eduard, *Socrates and the Socratic Schools*, tr. O. Reichel, London 1885 is a sample of the kind of philosophy Simmel was exposed to at the hands of his dean and dissertation supervisor.

INDEX